HISTORIC SC

FORTRESS SCOTLA
AND THE JACOBITES

HISTORIC ✶ SCOTLAND

FORTRESS SCOTLAND AND THE JACOBITES

CHRIS TABRAHAM AND DOREEN GROVE

B. T. Batsford Ltd / Historic Scotland

Typeset by DP Press Ltd
and printed in Great Britain by The Bath Press, Bath

Published by B. T. Batsford Ltd
4 Fitzhardinge Street, London W1H 0AH

A CIP catalogue record for this book is available from the British Library

ISBN 0 7134 7484 X (limp)
0 7134 7483 1 (cased)

Contents

Illustrations

Colour Plates

Acknowledgements

We are very grateful to those who have helped us in writing this book; in particular, Tam Dalyell for his Foreword, David Breeze, Allan Carswell, Iain MacIvor and John Simpson for their invaluable comments, Margaret Wilkes and her very helpful and patient staff at the National Library of Scotland's Map Library, Stephen Wood and his staff at the Scottish United Services Museum, Chris Unwin and Dave Pollock for their illustrations, David Henrie, Joseph White and Mike Brooks of Historic Scotland's photographic unit, Abbot Mark Dilworth and the brethren at Fort Augustus Abbey for their memorable guided tour, and Peter Kemmis Betty and Charlotte Kilenyi of Batsford for their encouragement. In addition, we are indebted to the years of research undertaken by Bruce Lenman without which any study of this period would be the poorer. Despite all their help, we accept full responsibility for all that we have written here.

We are also indebted to the following individuals and institutions for photographs for which they own the copyright: Her Majesty The Queen: The Royal Collection (65, 70, colour plates 10 and 15), His Grace the Duke of Roxburghe (5), His Grace the Duke of Buccleuch (8), the Earl of Mar (33), National Library of Scotland (28, 32, 41, 48, 50, 55–6, 58–9, 69, 72–3, 77, 80, 82, colour plates 3–4, 6, 8 and 13), National Trust for Scotland (6), National Galleries of Scotland (18, 24, 35, 52, colour plate 7), Queen's Own Highlanders Regimental Museum, Fort George (88), British Library (1, 12, 51, colour plate 2), British Museum (back cover), Maurice Scott Cameron (92), Royal Commission on the Ancient and Historical Monuments of Scotland (2), Tate Gallery (3), Provost and Fellows of Worcester College, Oxford (4), Public Record Office (81), Strathmore Estates (16), National Museums of Scotland (23), Trustees of the Blairs College Museum, Aberdeen and City of Aberdeen Art Gallery and Museum's Collection (27), E.T. Archive; private collection (36), Scottish Record Office (15, 61), National Portrait Gallery, London (66) and the BBC and Hulton Picture Library (68).

All the remaining illustrations are copyright Historic Scotland.

Foreword

by Tam Dalyell, MP

Between 1950 and 1952, like most of my generation, I did two years National Service. It must strike any of us in our sixties that the military ambience in which we served bears an affinity with the fascinating and scholarly description of service life, pictured by Chris Tabraham and Doreen Grove; I take just one delicious excerpt from the book relating to the latter half of the seventeenth century:

> Pay was miserable. An ordinary infantryman was paid just over 2p a day (5d), a foot guardsman $2\frac{1}{2}$ p (6d) and a trooper $8\frac{1}{2}$ p (1s 8d), while by far the best paid were the horsemen from the King's Troop, rewarded with a respectable $12\frac{1}{2}$ p (2s 6d). As ever, the cavalry came off better than the infantry. Not unexpectedly, this was not clear profit for the soldier; stoppages for uniforms and food frequently reduced the wages to next to nothing.

> Discipline was maintained by regular use of punishments. For example, a soldier discovered sounding an alarm in camp without good reason 'shall be punished by riding a Wooden-horse or otherwise at the discretion of the Commander'; or should he fail to respond to a call to arms he 'shall either be clapped in irons for it, or suffer such other punishment, as a court-martial shall think fit'. For drunkenness 'whilst he should have been upon duty, he shall suffer death'. A harsh life indeed.

Yet, as an insight into a vanishing world of my youth, now vanished, I found Chris Tabraham and Doreen Grove's account simply entrancing. Indeed, I believe that the Army of 1950, in B.A.O.R., was closer in its mores to the army of 1750 than to that of 1995. Today, relatively junior members of the Army are in charge of high-technology equipment running into millions of pounds. Any teacher leading an expedition of school pupils, or parent on a day's outing to one of Scotland's military sites would be well-advised to obtain a copy, and side-line relevant nuggets from the voluminous information. There is an old Indian saying: 'You cannot understand a person unless you walk for a day in his mocassins'! Thus to understand my ancestor General Tam Dalyell of the Binns (see 6), the senior commander of the Tsar's armies 1656–66 and raiser of the Royal Scots Greys, it helps to live in his house, which has been transformed from ancient fortification to fortified building to dwelling house, the epicentre of a domestic estate. What my wife and I find enthralling about this book is that the wealth of material about the nuts and bolts, equipment and resources of the army illustrates the lives of soldiers and commanders as people.

Tam Dalyell

Introduction

If they [the Highlanders] *lay by we can not root them out and to provoke them and leave them in despair will make them call for these assistances from France.*

(Viscount Stair to the Duke of Hamilton, July 1691, in the immediate aftermath of the first Jacobite Rising)

Among the fine collection of Board of Ordnance maps and plans in the National Library of Scotland is a map of Scotland dated 1731 and signed C. Lemprière. This absorbing illustration was drawn up primarily to show how the various clans had lined up during the 1715 Jacobite Rising, whether for or against George I's Government, and in what numbers. C. Lemprière was most probably Clement Lemprière, who joined the Board of Ordnance, the body responsible for the construction, upkeep and repair of military structures, in 1716, the year the Rising collapsed, and who rose to become their chief draughtsman, based in the Tower of London, shortly before the last Rising in 1745. In addition to showing the disposition, loyalties and strengths of the various clans, Lemprière highlighted the locations of the principal government garrisons. These included the chief medieval royal castles of Edinburgh, Stirling, Dumbarton and Inverness as well as the more recent forts – Fort William and Fort Augustus – and barracks – Bernera, Inversnaid, Kiliwhimen and Ruthven.

This book tells the story of these places during a century (1650–1750) which was amongst the most troubled in Scotland's history. It began with Cromwell's invasion of Scotland and ended with the bloody field of Culloden, the last battle fought on British soil. It was a century that saw the downfall of the Stuart dynasty and the emergence of a Hanoverian one. It also witnessed the Union of the Parliaments of Scotland and England, in 1707.

A century of almost uninterrupted civil strife meant that Scotland required to look to its defences more closely than its southern neighbour. The mighty royal castles, perched on their lofty volcanic outcrops, were clothed in 'state-of-the-art' artillery defences, illustrating the painful struggle by military engineers to adapt such intractable sites to contemporary defensive needs; their interiors were remodelled to suit the changed accommodation requirements. New garrison forts and barracks were built in strategic locations to counter the new threats. And just as important as the buildings were the men who defended them, lived in them and marched forth from them. This book is as much the story of the emergence and evolution of the standing army as it is of the standing buildings.

There is one oddity about Clement Lemprière's splendid map – the Roman fort at Ardoch, in Perthshire, is highlighted in red. As far as the authors are aware, there was no construction work undertaken at Ardoch by the Hanoverian Government; neither was there any use made of those ancient defences by the Jacobites. In fact, Ardoch had no place in the events of that troubled century, it had no place on Lemprière's map, and it has no place in this book. So what was in Lemprière's mind when he highlighted Ardoch? Was he perhaps drawing an analogy between his own imperial majesty's attempt to subjugate the troublesome Highland clans and the much earlier conquest of the ancient tribes by imperial Rome? This evocation of the Roman spirit was evidently in the forefront of the mind of Lieutenant-General Wade, one of the central figures in this book. In an inscription on his cherished bridge over the River Tay near Aberfeldy, just 25 miles north of Ardoch, Wade recalls with pride:

> Admire this military way which extends for 250 miles beyond the Roman frontiers, striding over deserts and marshes, cutting through rocks and mountains, and crossing the impatient Tay. George Wade, prefect of the forces in Scotland, completed this arduous work in the year 1733, by his cleverness and the immense labours of his soldiers. See what the royal protection of George II is worth!

The awesome banks and ditches of Ardoch (**1**) were certainly the most potent and tangible symbol of the Roman occupation of Scotland next to the Antonine Wall itself; as the relics of the Hanoverian Government's occupation of 'North Britain' have in their turn become today.

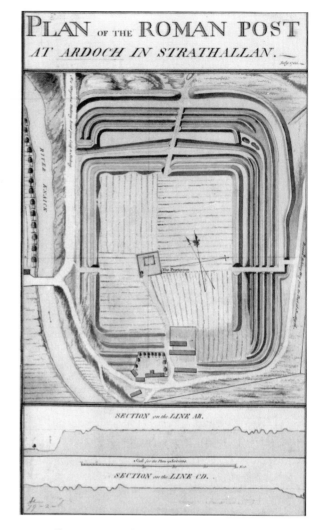

1 *William Roy's plan of the impressive Roman fort at Ardoch, dated 1755.*

CHAPTER ONE

From Castles to Forts

This fort formerly contributed much to keep the Highlands in subjection to the Government and intire peace amongst themselves.

(Captain John Slezer, Charles II's engineer, commenting on the citadel built at Inverlochy by Cromwell in 1654)

A new fort in the glen

On 14 May 1690 a squadron of warships and merchantmen sailing under the flag of William of Orange set sail from the busy Clyde port of Greenock bound for the western Highlands. Stored deep in the holds, beneath the feet of Major Ferguson's 800 troops, were materials for a new fort to be built in Lochaber.

Meanwhile, from his quarters safe within the garrison fortress of Edinburgh Castle, the instigator of the scheme, Major-General Hugh Mackay of Scourie, the commander of William's Scottish army, planned his next move – a forced march into Lochaber, where the main Jacobite disaffection lay, from Aberdeen by way of Strathdon and the Spey. It was a tremendous gamble, for in order to enter Lochaber in strength he would have to leave the rest of Scotland ill-defended. On 3 July Mackay, together with some 7000 troops, met up with the fleet at Inverlochy, at the head of Loch Linnhe. Almost immediately, work began on the construction of the new fort. Eleven days later, the garrison of 1200 men marched into their new quarters. Mackay named it Fort William in honour of his king. Meanwhile, the remainder of the country remained quiet; Mackay's gamble had paid off.

The plan for an impregnable base in Lochaber was nothing new. Indeed, Fort William was raised over the foundations of an older fort – Inverlochy Citadel – built at the mouth of the River Nevis by Cromwell's men in 1654. And just a short distance to the north, close to where the River Lochy entered Loch Linnhe, stood the imposing medieval Inverlochy Castle itself (**2**), from where the Red Comyn lords held sway over the inhabitants of Lochaber in the late thirteenth century.

There was a world of difference between the 'new' Fort William and the 'old' Inverlochy Castle. This was not because of any changes that had occurred locally; far from it. The western Highlands were just as ungovernable in the late seventeenth century as they had been five hundred years before. No. It was the nature of society that had altered during that time, and with it the science of warfare.

Medieval castles

Castles like Inverlochy were built primarily as residences for members of the landed nobility – the medieval predecessors of the great country houses of the modern era. But they were much more than that. The feudal obligations of a medieval landed nobleman

2 *Inverlochy Castle and Ben Nevis in 1849; by Michel Bouquet. The medieval lords held sway over the inhabitants of Lochaber from this mighty thirteenth-century castle until the seventeenth century.*

meant that his castle had to be capable of serving a number of additional functions: guest house, estate office, law court and prison – and, of course, stronghold.

To contrive a building which served acceptably both as residence and as fortress was asking an awful lot of a medieval mason-architect, but somehow he achieved it. But the priority was always to provide the lord with a suitably impressive house. The likes of Inverlochy were not hastily thrown up in times of war; they were carefully raised in times of peace, when lords had the finance, and their mason-architects the time, to build what were major construction works. Yes, castles had to be secure fastnesses, capable of withstanding siege when called on, but their lofty walls and

mighty towers were designed more to impress those who gazed upon them, friend and foe alike – statements in stone of their owners' wealth and standing in society.

The western Highlands had its fair share of castles. Many stand today, and even in ruin they are arresting spectacles in an equally compelling landscape. The Red Comyns at Inverlochy, the senior line of one of Scotland's most powerful families in the thirteenth century, were lords also of Badenoch. Their castle there sat atop the isolated hillock now occupied by Ruthven Barracks. Their neighbours to the west were the MacDougalls of Lorne. Although not as powerful or as wealthy, these descendants of Somerled (d. 1164) were nevertheless equally determined to build impressive fortress-residences, most notably Dunollie and Dunstaffnage.

The dramatic fall from power of both the Comyns and the MacDougalls during the wars with England in the first half of the fourteenth century simply led to their places being taken by three new noble families. The Campbells came to dominate mainland Argyll, with major castles at Inveraray and Kilchurn (**colour plate 1**); the MacDonalds' power-base were the Argyllshire islands, with seats at Finlaggan and Mingary; the MacRuaries, the least-known of the three, ruled over a scattered territory further north, from Moidart to Harris, from their base at Castle Tioram. These 'sons of Somerled' were of ancient Hebridean stock, unlike the Norman Comyns, but they were no less reluctant to embrace feudalism for that. Their great stone castles, amongst the most sophisticated in all Scotland, are testimony to that.

From these castles, then, were the inhabitants of the western Highlands controlled for the best part of five hundred years. Here they came to pay their rents, to receive justice and to gather round their lord in times of strife. But during the course of the seventeenth century two factors combined to change all that – the supremacy of the gun over conventional weapons, and the establishment of a regular army.

Guns

The new-fangled gun first appeared in Scotland by the early fifteenth century but two hundred years elapsed before it finally achieved supremacy over conventional artillery, like stone-throwing machines and cross-bows. The early guns, great bombards or siege guns like Mons Meg (presented to James II in 1457 and still proudly on display in Edinburgh Castle), were unpredictable and just as much a threat to those firing them as those being fired upon – as James II himself found to his cost at the siege of Roxburgh Castle in 1460 when a gun 'brak in the fyring' and fatally wounded him. Even so, shortly before the king's tragic death the first attempt to provide a purpose-built defence against the new technology had been made – by the mighty Earl of Douglas at his island fastness of Threave Castle, in Galloway.

The sixteenth century saw a great advance both in the effectiveness of the gun and in the siege-craft required to counter its growing threat. On the one hand, the gun foundries in the royal castles at Edinburgh and Stirling were gaining a reputation as centres of excellence. On the other, the 'Rough Wooing' of the mid-century provided the perfect opportunity for Scots, English and French alike to develop the theory of artillery fortification in a real theatre of war.

Little remains of the forts built in the south and east of the country during the 1540s and 1550s, but from what survives at Roxburgh Castle and Eyemouth, and from what we know from contemporary plans, it is clear that the latest principles of fortification were being followed. These turned their back completely on the principles which had determined the nature of castles – lofty stone walls – and adopted a much lower profile, relying on enormously thick mounds of earth. The projecting, tall, circular stone towers of the medieval castle were similarly replaced by squat, angular earthen bastions. Such were the defences that would soak up the punishment meted out by the murderous horizontal trajectory of the gun.

This left castle owners with a big problem. There they were behind their high stone walls, once thought impregnable but now so vulnerable. What were they to do? They might tinker at the edges – by punching gun-holes through the walls, as the Campbells did at Dunstaffnage, or piling earth onto the battlements in an attempt to soak up enemy bombardment, as the garrison at Inverlochy chose to do. But short of demolishing their ancient seats and building afresh, there was little they could practically do.

In the event they did not need to go to the trouble and expense. Society was changing, albeit slowly, and one by one the feudal burdens of a superior were being lifted from his shoulders by a royal government under King James VI determined to interfere more in

15

local community affairs. In the early seventeenth century, for example, responsibility for law and order had largely been taken over by the shire courts and the need for a lord to provide a law court and prison had been removed. More fundamentally, by the mid-century the notion of a regular army had taken root, a change which effectively rendered castles redundant as strongholds.

Oliver's army

On 22 July 1650, Oliver Cromwell marched into Scotland at the head of a 16,000 strong army (3). English armies had tramped this route often enough before, but this army was different. The Protector's troops were well drilled, well disciplined – and paid. His New Model Army was the first permanent military force to be seen in Britain. It was the beginning of a new era in soldiering.

Hitherto, armies had been created from the 'host' – ordinary working men of fighting age obligated to fight for their country for up to 40 days in any one year. When they were not fighting, they were at their homes, going about their normal business and living with their families. The creation of the English Parliament's New Model Army in 1645 changed all that, and when Charles II returned to his throne in 1660 he persisted with the idea, albeit in a modest way initially, and created a

3 Cromwell and his New Model Army at the Battle of Dunbar, 1650; by Andrew Gow. A cavalier officer was reported to have remarked to his opposite in the roundhead army: 'In our army we have the sins of men, drinking and wenching, but in yours you have those of the devil's, spiritual pride and rebellion.'

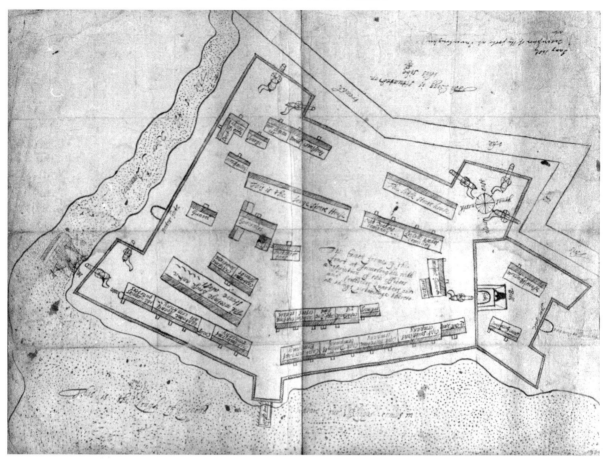

4 *A plan of the Cromwellian citadel at Inverlochy made in 1656 (from the Clarke papers). The similarity between this plan to the later Fort William (see* **colour plate 3***) suggests that Mackay largely rebuilt the old citadel. The postern gate visible on the ground today (see* **22***) is in precisely the same position as that marked on this plan.*

Standing Army.

Regular soldiers required more regular accommodation than did the old feudal host and Cromwell's troops in Scotland were soon garrisoned in purpose-built artillery forts, called citadels, drawn around the country like a noose – at Ayr, Perth (then called St Johnstons) and Inverness, all started in 1652, Inverlochy, begun in 1654 (**4**) and Leith, begun in 1655. Each citadel was different – in size and shape and contents. But they all conformed to a basic formula, incorporating the latest state-of-the-art bastioned defences while providing barracks and other accommodation. The minister of Kirkhill, writing in 1655, described the citadel at Inverness thus:

It was five-cornered with bastions, with a wide trench that an ordinary barque might sail in at full tide; the breast-work three storeys, built all of hewn stone limed within, and a brick wall. Centinel houses of stone at each corner, a sally-port to the south leading to the town, and on the north a great entry or gate called the Port, with a strong drawbridge of oak, called the Blue Bridge...this bridge was drawn evry night, and a strong guard within...In the centre of the citadel stood a great four-square building, all hewn stone, called the magazine and granary. In the third storey was the church, well furnished with a stately pulpit and seats, a wide bartizan at top, and a brave great clock with four large gilded dials and a curious ball...North-west and north-east are lower storeys for ammunition, timber, lodgings for manufactories, stablings, provision and brewing houses, and a great long tavern.

These new citadels were the shape of things to come, and castles a thing of the past. It was not quite the end for the castle, though. The great royal castles – Stirling, Edinburgh, Dumbarton, Inverness, and to a lesser extent Blackness – continued to serve as important garrison strongholds for some considerable time to come. Other ancient baronial castles were pressed into service as outposts to the main citadels by Cromwell's generals, among them Dunstaffnage, Dunollie and Ruthven,

and these and other castles across the Highlands were to be used as such throughout the period of the Jacobite troubles. But they no longer had an effective role in warfare; nor were they needed in peace-time any more. If those members of the landed class still residing in castles by 1660 were still worrying about how to meet the threat posed by the gun, then the establishment of a regular army got them off the hook; there no longer was any need for them to live behind their closed-up shells. It is surely more than coincidence that the last defensive house built in Scotland – Leslie Castle in Aberdeenshire – was erected in 1661, the very year the first regiments of horse and foot were formally embodied into the Scottish Army.

CHAPTER TWO

In Good King Charles's Golden Days

...and thair wes none in airmes in all Scotland, aither native or stranger, except the leiff gaird [life guard] fo his Majesteis use and weill of his subjects.

(John Nicoll, in his *Diary of Public Transactions*, 1662)

Cromwell's legacy

As General Monck's Commonwealth army marched south in 1660 to lay down its arms before the newly restored king, it left behind a profound legacy in Scotland. While few had welcomed Cromwell's invasion a decade earlier, some had been pleased that 'a man may ride all Scotland over with a switch in his hand and £100 in his pocket, which he could not have done these 500 years'. But the price of this peace was high. It took an occupying army of 36,000 men to achieve, and a policing force of 10,000 men to maintain.

In order to control the largely hostile Scots Cromwell adopted a two-pronged approach. Firstly, he knew it was not possible to suppress Scotland, and the Highlands in particular, without the support or at least the cooperation of a good proportion of the lairds and clan chiefs and so a new system of Justices of the Peace was created. The other element of the pacification was a stroke of military genius: the building of those five citadels, enabling the army numbers to be reduced whilst retaining a firm grip on an unhappy and often rebellious country. Monck

himself wrote of Inverlochy that it was 'a great deale of benefit to your highnesse, besides the securitie of the place and the advantage wee may have by laying fewer men there, if any troubles should be'.

The citadels may have been exorbitantly expensive, indeed they may never have been finished, but they provided an invaluable lesson, not only to the Scots but to a generation of military tacticians and engineers. They were strategically well placed to dominate as well as to defend. In Monck's own words, Leith Citadel was there to 'keepe in awe the chief citty of this nation'. Their architects, Hane, Rosworm, Van Dalem and Tessin, were regarded as the technical experts of their day, and it was in Scotland that they produced some of their best work. Each successive attempt to tighten the military noose around Scotland looked to the Cromwellian example of menacing fortresses in the very cradle of disaffection, the Highlands, supported by garrisons in the Lowland royal strongholds. Few countries are so well provided as Scotland with fortifications of aggression rather than defence.

The Protectorate Army which the citadels sheltered was also exceptional. Its structure, discipline and organisation led to its name, the New Model Army. The soldiers were well trained, most had first-hand experience of war, and they were adequately armed. They were also uniformly dressed, most in the coats of 'Venetian Red', which had become standard and which they bequeathed to the later British Army. The English Parliament had laid down the *Laws and Ordinances of War established for the better conduct of the army* as early as 1642, because although this was supposed to be an army with a common cause and interest, who believed they had God's might on their side, discipline was always a serious consideration. Interestingly, in this egalitarian army service medals were distributed to all ranks, for the first time in British history, after the crucial Battle of Dunbar in 1650 (*see* **3**).

Scotland's first standing army

The 'Restoration' of Charles II to his English throne was orchestrated by General George Monck (**5**). Charles had been crowned King of Scots on the Moot Hill at Scone on Ne'er Day

5 *King Charles II and his courtiers walking in Horse Guards Parade, London; by Hendrick Dankerts. In the background are the king's Guards and Garrison.*

1651 but it was his return in 1660 that heralded the return of royal control in both countries. His reign was very different from his father's. Charles II was largely indifferent to the running of Scotland and allowed its nobility to make the running. In addition, although he did not have his father's knack of riding straight into trouble, his reign was blighted by the constant strife with Covenanting dissenters. That dissent broke out into open hostility more than once during his reign. He had inherited a nation that was religiously divided and seriously war weary. Power in Scotland had shifted onto the shoulders of many of the very men who had opposed his father; indeed certain members of his new Privy Council had served during the Commonwealth.

In 1660, Charles II inherited a Scottish army of about 2000 men, formed from the remnants of the New Model Army and the companies of soldiers who had served in the various conflicts abroad. This standing army was the king's to command. He was empowered to raise troops as and when he required and could, in theory at least, employ them for whatever purpose he

wished. This is the stark fact, but neither the Scottish nor English Parliaments ever officially sanctioned the standing army. But the authorities in both countries recognised the need for a defensive force and for this reason it was reluctantly accepted. Technically the peace-time army did not exist. It was seen as a section of the King's Household, giving the king a free hand in recruiting and employing his army – with one important constraint. He was obliged to ask the Privy Council for any additional funds necessary to raise troops – game, set and match to the Privy Council.

Scotland, England and Ireland had separate army establishments. Each was funded from the revenue of its country and had a separate administration directly responsible to the king. Charles, like every contemporary European monarch, considered a standing army as a requirement. He accepted that this meant carrying a formidable military establishment, but what he could not so easily find was the means to supply such an army. After years of crippling taxes it is hardly surprising that a reduction in the permanent military establishment was sought in Scotland. And this meant fortifications as well as regiments. The influence of London-based Scots, like John Maitland, Earl of Lauderdale, soon persuaded Charles that it was proper to 'raze it (Inverlochy) and the other forts erected in Scotland by that great wicked man', for not only were they symbols of his former power but also the Estates could not afford to maintain them. The instruction to disband the garrisons and slight the forts was given in 1660. But by the spring of 1662 the two regiments of foot and a troop of horse under the command of Major-General Morgan, mostly based in Leith, remained to be disbanded. There was the little matter of £30,000 of arrears due to them. The Privy Council appealed to Charles to pay the balance, and this he did, at least sufficiently to see the last of the troops depart for foreign service in the late spring of that year. The citadel at Leith was given to the Earl of Lauderdale, who promptly persuaded (some say blackmailed)

Edinburgh to buy it from him. Perth was gifted to the town magistrates, Inverness to the Earl of Murray, and Ayr to the Earl of Eglinton for services rendered.

The new aristocratic regime was determined to reduce its taxes even if it meant starving the army. However, a proclamation of the Privy Council in 1661 did reluctantly accept 'such forces both horse and foot as we consider necessary to prevent a suddain invasion'. The essence of all discussion in the Privy Council centred around the need to avoid expense. In 1663 the Estates offered to provide the king with a militia army of 20,000 foot and 2000 horse; to be 'sufficiently armed and furnished with forty days provision'. Charles refused the offer but the idea of a militia army continued to be mooted. But it was not until October 1678 that Charles agreed to select 5000 foot and 500 horse from those on offer, to provide a small but reliable force. It proved itself well in the Covenanters' rising that broke out in the following year.

In 1660 the Earl of Middleton was appointed as General of all Scottish forces. He had little support from the older Scots nobility and it was a very small army, consisting of two troops of horse, six companies of foot, supplemented by the garrisons in the royal castles of Stirling, Dumbarton and Edinburgh and a core of non-regimental officers. This last comprised: the muster-master general, Major Arnot; the commissary-general, Sir William Bruce; the physician, Christopher Irvine; the surgeon-major, John Jossey; the knight-marshall, Sir John Keith; the town major of Edinburgh Castle, Robert Johnston; and the adjutant-general, Matthew Hamilton. The overall cost to the Treasury was £32,000 a year. Middleton resigned in 1664 and his place was taken not by a soldier but by a politician, the Earl of Rothes, appointed because of his loyalty to the king.

The establishment of a standing army, however small, was a new departure for Scotland. It provided a new career for the nobility, many of whom were reeling from the financial ruin of the civil wars of the previous twenty years. Soldiering

6 General Tam Dalyell; a portrait by an unknown artist hanging in the Dining Room at The House of The Binns, near Linlithgow, the home of Tam and Kathleen Dalyell.

before the 1640s had been tied to the nobility's view of lordship and obligation, but by the Restoration the discipline of the command structure within the army was established and there was a pool of very experienced soldiers to draw upon. In addition to those who had served in the civil wars, thousands of Scots had served in Europe as mercenaries. Not surprisingly, professional soldiering appealed to the less-wealthy noblemen or the younger sons of great families – men like Alexander Leslie, Earl of Leven, General Thomas (Tam) Dalyell of the Binns (6), Sir John Keith and General Middleton. Patronage of such soldiers gave the Crown control over men who desired to become noble and over noblemen who needed jobs in the army.

The army establishment

At first, the army establishment was small: His Majesty's Troop of Guards under the captaincy of the Earl of Newburgh, Middleton's Troop of Horse and a regiment of His Majesty's Foot Guards raised in 1662, after the last of the English soldiers had left, and commanded by the Earl of Linlithgow. Added to that were a handful of companies of infantry and the garrisons in the royal castles. Edinburgh Castle had two companies, one commanded by Middleton and the other an independent company commanded by the Earl of Kellie. Dumbarton was commanded by the Duke of Lennox and Stirling by the Earl of Mar, hereditary keeper of the castle. In addition, there was the Company of Artillery under James Wemyss; from carpenter and undergunners up to the captain it was a force of less than 25 men.

The regimental system was by now well established, although it is the smaller divisions of the regiment that are of greater relevance in the Scottish army. Each regiment or smaller unit was known by the name of its commanding officer (a fact which makes following the career of a regiment difficult). Each regiment of foot consisted of about 1000 men, divided into ten companies. The field officers were a colonel, a lieutenant-colonel and a major, and each had charge of a company. The remaining companies had a captain in command (up to seven if the regiment was up to strength), a lieutenant as second-in-command and an ensign who carried the colours (the company flag). Below them was a varying number of sergeants and corporals, perhaps three or four of each, and two drummers. The staff of a regiment also varied but it usually included a quartermaster, a chaplain, a provost-marshal, a surgeon and his assistant. A cavalry regiment consisted of six troops of 60 men, with a similar proportion of officers to a troop as a company of foot, only replacing the ensign with a cornet and the drummers with trumpeters. In addition, a saddler and a farrier were required to deal with the horses. Several of the troops of horse were larger than 60. Middleton's Troop had 120 men and its replacement, raised by the Earl of Rothes, had 80.

Of the rank and file soldiers we know virtually nothing except that occasionally their names are given in the few muster rolls that survive. It is safe to assume that the personnel of the army were, as at all other times until the present century, drawn from the ranks of disillusioned young men seeking to avoid the

The old CITY GUARD of EDINBURGH.

drudgery of rural or urban poverty, or Highland youth obeying their clan chiefs. Clothing and food were supplied almost regularly, pay was promised (though in practice it was very little and often in arrears) and a bed of sorts would be found at the end of every day. Their lives were dictated by the *Orders for the conduct of the King's Forces,* issued in 1667 and reinforced by the *Articles and Rules for the Better Government of His Majesties Forces in Scotland*, introduced in 1675. Both were dominated by the importance of Divine Worship and an abhorrence of rebellion and indiscipline.

Pay was miserable. An ordinary infantryman was paid just over 2p a day (5d), a foot guardsman $2\frac{1}{2}$p (6d) and a trooper $8\frac{1}{2}$p (1s 8d), while by far the best paid were the horsemen from the King's Troop, rewarded with a respectable $12\frac{1}{2}$p (2s 6d). As ever, the cavalry came off better than the infantry. Not unexpectedly, this was not clear profit for the soldier; stoppages for uniforms and food frequently reduced the wages to next to nothing.

Discipline was maintained by regular use of punishments. For example, a soldier discovered sounding an alarm in camp without good reason 'shall be punished by riding a Wooden-horse (7) or otherwise at the discretion of the Commander';

7 *'Riding the horse', from John Kay's Caricatures.*

or should he fail to respond to a call to arms he 'shall either be clapped in irons for it, or suffer such other punishment, as a court-martial shall think fit'. For drunkenness 'whilst he should have been upon duty, he shall suffer death'. A harsh life indeed.

Uniforms were supplied. A soldier's kit comprised a cap, coat, breeches, stockings and shoes – all to be worn or carried in his 'snapsacks'. There were no regulation colours for any part of the uniform and many different coloured coats must have been seen. But a brief look through the records of cloth purchases made by the army at this time puts 'reid cloth' as the firm favourite. However, when General Dalyell raised his Regiment of Dragoons in 1681 he was unable to procure the quantity of stone-grey cloth he required in Scotland, so he sought permission to purchase the material abroad. This regiment was destined to become known as the Scots Greys.

The length of service was open ended, until either age, infirmity, disbandment – or death – forced retirement. At least some small help was at hand for those who were old or invalided. Charles II, emulating the French, built a hospital for the soldiers of the English army; for Scottish soldiers in similar circumstances he allowed a small pension.

The quartering of the army was a constant problem, both to the commanding officers and to those it was quartered on. The billeting laws in Scotland allowed the army to billet on private individuals. Indeed, billeting on sections of the community who had not been sufficiently diligent in paying their taxes became a common punishment – as the shires of Inverness, Sutherland, Orkney, Shetland and most of the shires in south-west Scotland all found to their cost. Even the garrison in Edinburgh Castle was sent to quarter on the good citizens of the city who were proving dilatory in paying their dues. In 1661 the cost of:

> … quartering and daylie allowance [was fixed by] the said Lords [of the Privy Council, who] doe allow to ilk horseman the soume of tuentie four shilling Scotts daylie or frie quarters at that rate and no more, and if they have received free quarter alreadie they are to have no money, and ordaines this to be for a constant ruell through the whole kingdom in tyme comming.

The numerical strength of the army changed little during Charles's reign. With the exception of those extra troops raised during the various emergencies, in particular the religious risings of 1666 and 1679 (8) following which they were immediately disbanded, it stayed around the 2000 mark. This was pathetically small to cover such a large geographical area or indeed to undertake the tasks and duties demanded of it.

8 *The Battle of Bothwell Brig, 1679, at which Charles II's army, led by his natural son the Duke of Monmouth, defeated the Covenanting army; by John Wyck.*

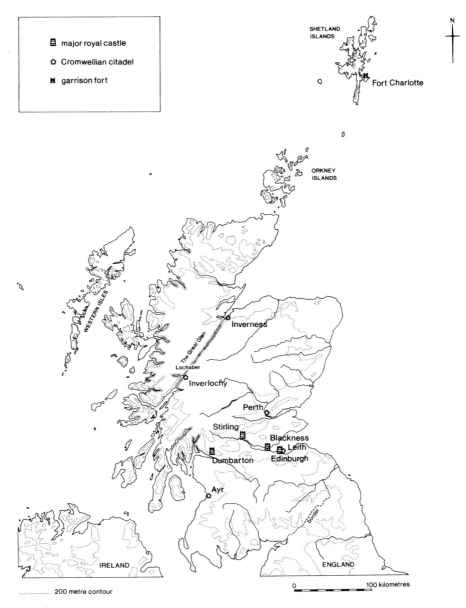

9 *The military places of strength in the latter half of the seventeenth century* (Chris Unwin).

The policing job alone required twice that number, but add to that the important tasks of manning the strong-points and garrisons and defending the country from external threat and it was clearly woefully inadequate.

Royal garrisons

The chief garrisons (**9**) were in the royal castles of Edinburgh, Stirling (**10**), Dumbarton and to a lesser degree Blackness. Each consisted of a small number of permanent staff – a captain or governor, supported by officers, gunners, soldiers and miners as well as storekeepers, wheelwrights and gunsmiths. This staff was supplemented by companies from the regiments of guards. Between them they had the job of protecting the major places of strength. Edinburgh Castle was the home of the Scottish Command, with its general

25

10 *Stirling Castle from the south-east.*

officers, the major-general of the forces, the physician-general and the adjutant-general. The governors were often absentees, pursuing other military and political duties. When General Middleton resigned as governor of Edinburgh Castle in 1664 the Earl of Lauderdale took over his post. Before the Restoration 'the Captaines and Keepers of the Castells, haveing great fees and allowances for keeping the same, ought to have no allowance for the watchmen and soldiers'. Fortunately for the later keepers this rule was relaxed and although they were still responsible for the pay of the garrisons they were reimbursed, in theory at least!

With the slighting of the citadels at Inverlochy and Inverness there was no longer a government stronghold in the Highlands. It became apparent early on in Charles's reign that the Highlands were considered too great a task to even consider taking seriously. Despite constant calls to the Privy Council to reinstate a garrison at Inverlochy no action was taken. In 1664 forty musketeers from the King's Foot Guards were ordered to be stationed there, 'the chiefs in the neighbourhood being charged to provide these troops with fire and bedding'. Their instructions were to secure peace in the Highlands against 'herships, theiftes, robers and depredations daylie commited upon His Majesties peacable and obedient subjects'. But such a pitiable number was never going to solve the problem. Nor was there any determined attempt to solve the problem from within, as the English had attempted to do, with some success, during the Protectorate. In 1667 the Earl of Atholl was given a commission to raise independent companies to 'keep watch upon the braes' and other such companies were to follow (like the two companies of foot raised in 1678 by Sir James Campbell of Lawers and Colonel James Menzies for 'securing the peace of the Highlands', but they proved difficult to control and as unpredictable as their leaders).

The task of constructing and maintaining the barrack buildings and artillery fortifications at the royal garrisons fell to the king's master-mason, a long-established post. Charles II's master-mason was Robert Mylne, after whom Mills (or Mylne's) Mount Battery in Edinburgh Castle might possibly be named. But the work was carried out in a very *ad hoc* way, with no overall strategy and only when a weakness was perceived and the Privy Council were persuaded to vote the required funds.

Mylne's biggest task for the army authorities was the building of a fort in Shetland as part of the defence of the realm following the re-opening of hostilities against the Dutch in 1665. This fort, which was finally completed over a century later and renamed Fort Charlotte in honour of George III's queen, proved to be the only new fortification to be built in Scotland during Charles's reign (**11**).

The anchorage in Bressay Sound was an important safe haven for the king's navy and the fort was built ostensibly to help defend the sound from a Dutch attack. But the doubtful loyalties of the Shetlanders may also have contributed to the decision for they were thought to have a 'greater affection to the Dutch than they have either to Scots or to English'. Lord Rothes, who made this charge, was despatched to Lerwick to assess the situation. He found that all the best sites for a fort were overlooked by high ground to the landward and that the soil was so thin that he doubted if it would be possible to build the bastions. But a site was chosen and

Mylne was instructed to draw up designs. He chose to adopt the style favoured by Cromwell's military architects – a roughly pentagonal, bastioned defence with a zigzag parapet wall facing out over the bay. Inside was a two-storey barrack block for 100 men. Outside was a 'Cellar call'd powder Room', presumably to remove the danger of accidental explosion from the interior of the fort, but thereby creating an additional danger if the fort was ever besieged.

The occupying garrison was commanded by Colonel Sinclair who bemoaned the 'smalle Gunns & the greatest but demi culverines soe too smalle for the batteries towards the sea or Sownd, neither have they balle ffor those they have'. Luckily for him and his men, when a Dutch fleet of 24 sail was sent to capture Shetland in June 1667 its commander, Admiral Van Ghent, had been misinformed that Governor Sinclair had a regiment of 1000 men and a fort bristling with 40 guns. Perhaps if Van Ghent had been able to see the fort more clearly through the mist he might not have been so easily put off. By this date the earthworks of the fort were in a good condition, well defended by palisades and stockades, but little progress had been made on building the stone walls for lack of lime and workmen. Doubts were already beginning to form as to the wisdom of finishing the fort and maintaining it. King Charles wanted it completed and given a permanent garrison of 40–50 men, but the Treaty of Breda concluding this Second Dutch War, signed in July 1667, proved the death knell. By November Charles had accepted that the cost was too high and ordered the Privy Council to disband the garrison, remove the arms and slight the fortifications. It had cost about £28,000 sterling in two years. During the Third Dutch War (1672–7) the abandoned fort was not garrisoned and when the Dutch landed in 1673 they burnt the barrack block and a number of other buildings in the town. Two years earlier another arrival from the Low Countries was to prove far more beneficial to the Scots.

11 *The south gate into Fort Charlotte, a legacy from the fort begun but left incomplete in 1665–7. The gate was reduced in size to allow only pedestrian access when the fort was rebuilt in the 1780s.*

Captain John Slezer

John Slezer arrived in the country late in 1671 to take up the post of chief engineer to the Artillery Train, holding the rank of lieutenant. Now for the first time a permanent professional hand was laid on the Scottish guards and garrisons, drawing together the disparate disciplines of architecture, engineering and gunnery.

Slezer may have been a Dutchman. He was certainly of northern European origin, though he described himself only as 'foreign', and that is all that can be firmly established. His early training as a military engineer was in the Netherlands for the House of Orange, where he was clearly given an excellent grounding in design and surveying techniques as well as in the practical problems of building and maintaining fortifications and their associated artillery. Slezer recounts how:

> being upon my travels in the year 1669, I came to Scotland, where I met with great civilities and especially from the late Earls of Argyll and Kincardine, to whome I had the

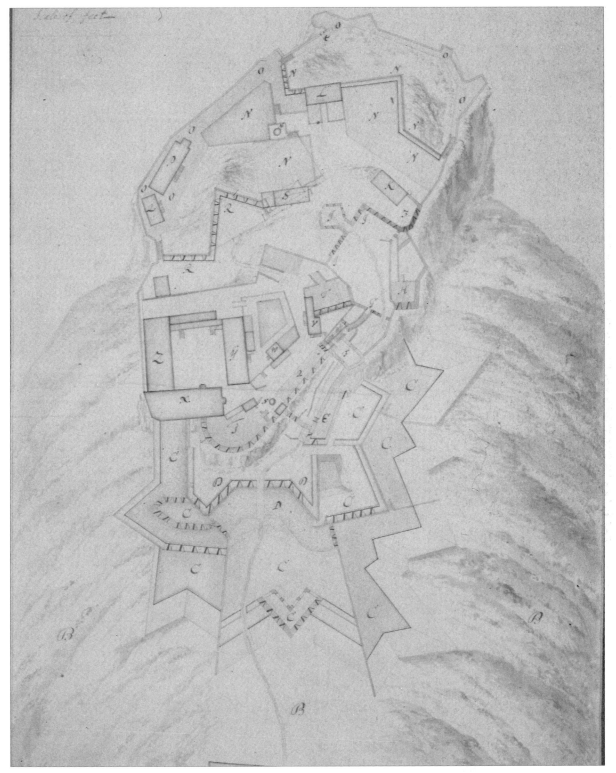

12 *John Slezer's planned improvements to both the defences and the internal buildings of Edinburgh Castle. Although undated, the plan was probably drawn soon after his arrival in Scotland in 1671.*

honour to become particularly known. I had their lordships favour to that degree, that they proposed I should be employed here, but no occasion then offering I left the Kingdom. Three years thereafter I had letters from them most kindly inviting me to embrace a post in the army they had procured for me.

Slezer's first task was to draw up for Charles Maitland of Hatton, the Treasurer Depute, plans for the repair and improvement of Edinburgh Castle (**12**). These are now the earliest surviving plans of Scottish fortifications drawn up using accurate survey methods. In addition to his role as engineer the king

awarded Slezer a warrant as the lieutenant of the Artillery Train. This document not only explains Slezer's own job but also gives us a remarkable insight into the organisation of the garrison system at the time. It is worth quoting from extensively:

First, he is to make a trial of his skill in artillery and fireworks at the King's charge before them as soon as he conveniently can and for that end they are to cause to be erected for him a laboratory or working house in Edinburgh Castle.

Secondly, they are to signify to the Earl of Linlithgow and the Governors of the Castles of Edinburgh, Stirling and Dumbarton that the said Slezar choose one man out of each company of the Regiment of Guards, five out of the garrison of Edinburgh, three out of that of Stirling Castle and two out of that of Dumbarton to instruct and train them in all

13 *Blackness Castle from the south-west with the Spur in the foreground. The upper part of the Spur, with its square gun embrasures, crenellated parapet and round sentinel turret, dates from the 1690s.*

things belonging to artillery as gunnery, casting hand grenadoes and fireworks, and that the said Slezar shall have full command over those 20 men till they be perfectly instructed and then he is to choose others as he shall see cause.

Thirdly, that all the gunners in the forts, garrisons and land forces are to obey the said Slezar as the King's lieutenant of artillery in all things relating to his office.

Fourthly, that all gunners that shall be hereafter placed in forts, garrisons and land forces shall be examined and approved by the said Slezar.

Fifthly, that he signify to them what gunners, cannons, mortar pieces, grenades and all other instruments and materials of artillery he shall think fit to transport from one place or garrison to another, and that they give him their warrant for their transportation and particularly what great brass gunns he shall think fit to transport from Dumbarton Castle to Edinburgh Castle.

Sixthly, that he make an inventory of all guns and other materials belonging to the artillery and signify to them what carriages or other necessary things are wanting.

Seventhly, that he provide all things which the King shall think fit hereafter to be added to the artillery and they give hime their warrant for it from time to time, he being always accountable to them in every thing.

Eighthly, that he shall visit all castles and garrisons at least twice a year, and report to them of his diligence for which end they are to give order that he be provided with convenient lodging in all the forts and castles.

Slezer's twin roles – as chief engineer responsible for the design and repair of fortifications, and as lieutenant of the Artillery Train – put him in a singular position. For 46 years he stayed at the helm and during that time he made his presence felt. He supervised building works at all the royal garrisons, and although much of his work was replaced during the years of Jacobite

disaffection in the early decades of the following century, considerable remains can still be seen at Blackness (the upper part of the Spur, a gun battery flanking the entrance (**13**)), Dumbarton (the Spur Battery, again covering the main entrance) and Edinburgh. His proposals for Edinburgh Castle outlined in his early plans demonstrate an ability to understand the needs both of the architecture and of the men who were to use it (**colour plate 2**). Perhaps the best legacy of Slezer's work is to be seen here, in the perimeter wall wrapped around the Upper Ward, loopholed for light artillery and muskets and pierced by the enigmatically named Foog's Gate, beside which the great medieval bombard, Mons Meg, was unceremoniously dumped in 1681.

No longer there for us to admire, but no less important for that, was Slezer's development of the Artillery Train which he saw mature from a small number of gunners to an established hierarchy of gunners, practitioner gunners, bombardiers, petardiers and miners. The introduction of specialist training to the guards and garrisons as well as to gunners showed vision and could only improve the overall effectiveness. He also presided over an expansion of the engineering services. His appointment as engineer in 1671 may have been a personal appointment with no staff, but by the time of his death in 1717 there was an established department with a chief engineer, one engineer and at times two assistant engineers.

Slezer was a multi-talented man, and his work for the Government was merely his 'day job'. He is much better known today as the author of *Theatrum Scotiae*, 'a book of figures and draughts of all the King's Castles, Palaces, towns, and other notable places in the Kingdom belonging to private subjects' (**14**). This work must have taken up a great deal of time, but he was no doubt helped by the eighth clause in his warrant which required him to travel around the kingdom at the Government's expense.

Money was to be Slezer's downfall. *Theatrum Scotiae* never repaid the production costs and as with many army officers he spent his own money to supply his company. On several occasions he had to pay on 'Account of the cloathing Money due to the artillery company by reason that I was forced to engage personally for the payment of their Mounting or suffer my company to go naked'. The cumulative effects of the Government not paying its debts and *Theatrum Scotiae* not making a profit left Slezer bankrupt, forcing him to live for his last 14 years in the debtors' sanctuary in Holyrood. He continued to work, though, and signed his last muster roll for the Artillery Train, with a very shaky hand, in November 1717 (**15**). After his death, his widow and son continued to press the authorities for the payment of monies due but the parsimonious Government contrived to avoid doing so. It was an ignominious end to an illustrious career.

Despite the arrival of John Slezer, by King Charles's death in 1685 the only important mili-tary achievement which can be laid at his Scottish door was his tenacious determination to have and to hold a permanent standing army. Fiscal problems prevented him from adequately maintaining existing fortifications, never mind indulging in the luxury of innovation. But there was no longer any doubt that the king had the right to raise an army. Charles handed over to his younger brother, James VII, a permanent, if small, army supplemented by a sizeable militia.

James was not slow in ordering his troops into the field, and it was to the Highlands that they were despatched. Having earlier stirred up the deep-rooted hatred felt by the Catholic and Episcopalian west Highland clans towards the Protestant Campbells of Argyllshire, shortly after taking the throne James unleashed his army in a vicious assault on all those associated with the Earl of Argyll's abortive rising. Therein were sown the seeds for the half-century and more of Jacobite disaffection that was to follow the downfall of James himself three years later.

14 *John Slezer's prospect of Stirling Castle, from his* Theatrum Scotiae, *published in 1693.*

The Prospect of Sterling Castle

15 *A 1717 muster roll of the 'Artillery Company in North Britain' signed by John Slezer in a shaky hand.*

CHAPTER THREE

Revolution and Rising

I fought at land, I fought at sea,
At hame I fought my auntie-o
But I met the Devil, and Dundee
On the braes o' Killiecrankie-o.

(A verse from the folk song *The Braes o'*
Killiecrankie, celebrating the Jacobite
victory at the Battle of the Pass of
Killiecrankie, 1689)

Jacobites and Williamites

On 5 November 1688, Prince William of
Orange, son of Charles I's eldest daughter
Mary, with his wife Mary, James VII's eldest
daughter, landed at Torbay, on the south coast
of England. By Christmas Day, William and
Mary, now proclaimed joint sovereigns of
England, were in residence in St James's
Palace, London, whilst James VII, his wife
Mary and their infant son James, made their
way to Saint Germain-en-Laye, near Paris, and
exile. The episode is known in English history
as the 'Glorious Revolution'. For the Scots,
although they had had their difficulties with
King James, the revolution in England had
come as something of a surprise. They were
now faced with the question of who should
govern them, and the answer was by no means
so clear cut as it had been south of the Border.
When the Convention Parliament met in
Edinburgh on 14 March 1689 to debate the
issue, the house was equally divided between
'Jacobites' (from the Latin 'Jacobus' meaning

James) and 'Williamites'. When it ultimately
decided, on 4 April 1689, to offer the throne
of Scotland to William and Mary, 'Jacobitism'
was born as a political cause.

One significant factor in the Scottish equa-
tion was the predominance of the Catholic
and Episcopalian clans in the Highlands. This

16 *John Graham of Claverhouse, Viscount*
Dundee, the victor of Killiecrankie; the portrait
by Sir Godfrey Kneller hangs in the Great
Drawing Room at Glamis Castle.

wild and mountainous country had long proved a thorn in the side of the central government ruling from its eastern Lowland bases. Lawlessness and violence were seemingly endemic, and this was no more true than in the heart of Gaeldom, the western Highlands, where clans like the MacGregors, the Mac-Donalds of Keppoch and Glencoe and the Robertsons of Struan made banditry a way of life. 'A uhol country of robbers,' the Earl of Seaforth pronounced it in 1682; 'the greate theife holes of ye highlands,' wrote another. The clans' adherence to Catholicism and Episcopalianism was matched only by their undying hatred of the Protestant Clan Campbell, whose power-base was Argyll. When Archibald Campbell, 9th Earl of Argyll, attempted an abortive Protestant rising against the Catholic King James in 1685, the latter instructed: 'All men who joyned are to be killed or disabled ever from fighting again; and burn all houses except honest men's. Let the women and children be transported to remote Isles.' This ruthless edict against the Campbells may not have contributed much to the maintenance of law and order in the western Highlands but it did endear the Catholic clans to His Majesty and ensured their loyalty to him even after his flight to France.

Even before the Convention Parliament made its well-nigh unanimous decision to offer the Crown of Scotland to William and Mary, James's supporters had decided that their cause would not be won there. On 18 March, John Graham of Claverhouse, Viscount Dundee (**16**), the leader of the Jacobite group, left the Convention bent on raising support for his exiled monarch elsewhere. Before leaving for the north, Dundee conferred with the governor of Edinburgh Castle, the Duke of Gordon, at the sallyport on the Western Defences (**17**). Gordon, a devout Catholic, on hearing of Prince William's 'invasion', had vowed to preserve the castle 'for the King, though the Prince of Orange should obtain possession of every other fortress in the

17 *The postern gate on the western side of Edinburgh Castle where the two Jacobites, the Duke of Gordon and Viscount Dundee, conferred in March 1689 shortly before the first Rising.*

kingdom'. After seeing Dundee off, Gordon set about keeping his promise.

At that time the entire strength of the garrison numbered a little over 120 officers and men. They had no doctor, no engineer and less than 100 barrels of powder to fire 22 cannon. (The main magazine in Scotland had been transferred to Stirling Castle shortly before.) Ranged against them were the 800 men of the Earl of Leven's Regiment, newly raised for the purpose. (Leven's Regiment, known also as the Edinburgh Regiment, later became the 25th Regiment of Foot, in 1805 took the title of the King's Own Borderers and in 1887 became known as the King's Own Scottish Borderers,

18 *Major-General Hugh Mackay of Scourie, commander of William's Scottish Army and the founder of Fort William.*

by which the regiment is known today.) They were soon relieved by the three Scottish regiments of William's Dutch Brigade (Mackay's, Balfour's and Ramsey's) led by Major-General Hugh Mackay of Scourie himself (**18**), by now appointed General of William's Scottish Army.

Despite being seasoned troops, the besiegers failed to make any immediate impact on the garrison, and the siege dragged on for three weary months. 'The Besiegers constantly

19 *A makeshift cemetery containing at least 15 skeletons under excavation in Edinburgh Castle in 1989. The skeletons, all male, were probably soldiers serving in the garrison during the 1689 siege who had succumbed to disease whilst holed up in the dank casemates beneath the Half-Moon Battery* (Peter Yeoman and Steve Driscoll).

throw in their Bombs and other Fireworks into the Castle, tho often for whole days the garrison is so uncivil as not to return one Bullet.' Gordon, nervous about the loyalty of his men, dared not make sorties; neither would he fire on the city. Mackay, lacking heavy guns, failed to breach the defences of

20 *The military places of strength 1689–1714* (Chris Unwin).

this seemingly impregnable rocky fortress. The arrival of heavy mortars in April badly damaged the castle buildings and drove the garrison into the unhealthy but bomb-proof stone-vaulted casemates deep beneath the gun-platform of the Half-Moon Battery. Some of the garrison succumbed to disease and were buried there, and macabre illustration of this came recently, and unexpectedly, during archaeological excavations in 1989 when the

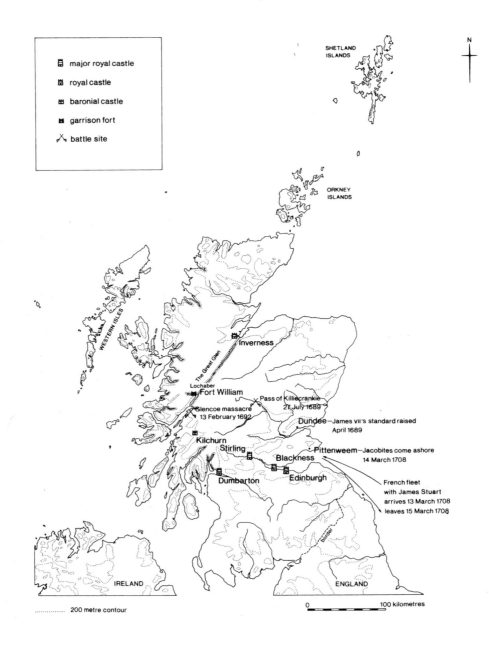

major royal castle

royal castle

baronial castle

garrison fort

battle site

SHETLAND ISLANDS

ORKNEY ISLANDS

N

WESTERN ISLES

Inverness

The Great Glen

Lochaber
Fort William

Glencoe massacre
13 February 1692

Pass of Killiecrankie
27 July 1689

Dundee—James VII's standard raised
April 1689

Kilchurn

Stirling

Pittenweem—Jacobites come ashore
14 March 1708

Blackness

Dumbarton

Edinburgh

French fleet
with James Stuart
arrives 13 March 1708
leaves 15 March 1708

IRELAND

ENGLAND

Border

200 metre contour

0   100 kilometres

skeletons of 15 young, able-bodied men were discovered in a hastily-made cemetery beside the castle's Inner Barrier (19). Their deaths were in vain for, on 13 June, Gordon and his remaining emaciated garrison of 50 surrendered.

As important as the taking of Edinburgh Castle was to the Williamites, their far more pressing priority was the suppression of the Jacobite Rising proclaimed when Viscount Dundee raised James VII's standard on Dundee Law in early April. After a cat-and-mouse chase through the Highlands by Dundee and Mackay – one contemporary wrote of 'Viscount Dundee, with his troop skipping from one hill to another, like wildfire' – the two finally met in battle at the Pass of Killiecrankie on 27 July. The confused loyalties of Scots generally is epitomised by this short-lived encounter: a Highlander leading an essentially Lowland army against a Highland army led by a Lowlander! The tragedy for the Jacobites was that they lost their gallant leader, 'Bonnie Dundee', in the very hour of his victory. The loss of this great soldier to the Jacobite cause removed any hope, for the time being, of their achieving success.

21 Fort William, Ben Nevis and the southern end of the Great Glen.

Fort William and Maryburgh (20)

Most of Dundee's 2000 troops at Killiecrankie had been recruited among the Catholic and Episcopalian west Highland clans. Lochaber, at the southern end of the Great Glen (21), was 'a good cradle for a rising', a fact acknowledged by Mackay when he pleaded with his king that he might be 'furnished with all materials necessary for the building of a Citadel at Innerlochy, for the better reducing of, and keeping the Highlanders in order'. The Convention Parliament, in July 1689, even passed a resolution to fortify Inverlochy: 'It is believed that it will the sooner be more effectuate, by reason of some Remains of Fortification that yet continue there, since the time the English were in those Parts and made Inverlochy the chief garrison, and head quarters in all those Highlands, which kept all the savage inhabitants in those countries in great awe, and forc'd them to live regularly, as their Lowland neighbours used to do.' This was nothing new. Numerous proposals had been made during Charles II's reign to rebuild Cromwell's citadel at Inverlochy 'for greater effectiveness against thieves' but all had foundered on the twin rocks of indifference and lack of money. Mackay's plan, too, met with a deafening silence from King William; the money and the

men were more urgently needed in Ireland. Then suddenly, on 1 March 1690, with the situation in Ireland deteriorating, and the spectre of the western Highlands erupting into open rebellion once again, Mackay got his money and his men. And so unfolded the events described at the beginning of chapter one and by 3 July Mackay was at Inverlochy supervising the construction of his new garrison fortress, named Fort William in honour of his king.

Mackay was not entirely happy reusing the English citadel: 'The situation of the old fort did not please me, being commanded from a near hill, but I could not change it, there being none else to fit.' The new fort was a rushed affair, virtually finished by the time Mackay departed for Stirling on 18 July: 'In 11 days I got it at its full height, the matter of 20 feet from the bottom of the fosse, pallisaded

22 *Fort William's north-west demi-bastion* (right) *and a stretch of the north rampart* (left). *The sallyport through the rampart may be a legacy from the Cromwellian citadel.*

round, with a *chemin couvert* [covered way] and glacis, a perfect defence.' What Mackay had supervised was the construction not of a great stone fort – that came only with time – but something little more than an earthwork with a wooden palisade on top – a 'trinch' one soldier called it. It followed pretty well the shape of its Cromwellian predecessor slighted in 1661 (see **4**): an irregular pentagon with a three-pointed bastion at the south-east and four two-pointed demi-bastions at the other corners. There were two entrance gates: the main gate mid-way along the south front, protected by a detached triangular earthwork or ravelin, and a sallyport (possibly a legacy from the Cromwellian citadel) through the north wall tucked in beside the north-west demi-bastion, and needing no additional frontal defence because of its proximity to the River Nevis and the boggy morass that dominated this side of the fort (**22**). The west side facing Loch Linnhe was equally safe from ground attack (though it was vulnerable to a sea-borne assault), and so the additional outer defences of the fort – the '*chemin couvert* and

23 *Soldiers under canvas in the 1730s* (Scottish United Services Museum).

glacis' mentioned by Mackay in his despatches – were restricted to the vulnerable south and east flanks.

As soon as the fort was completed, the 1200-strong garrison marched in, and 12 guns taken from the fleet anchored in Loch Linnhe were emplaced on the bastioned defences, the heavier pieces pointing out to sea in case of a French attack. The fort's first governor, Colonel John Hill, was like a ghost from the past returning to haunt the present for he had previously been in charge of Cromwell's citadel at Inverlochy.

The first few months were beset with problems. The men lived under canvas initially (**23**), an existence made even more uncomfortable by the deteriorating weather conditions and the lack of proper pay and provisions. Timber ('deals') arrived for the new barrack buildings but no nails! And Mackay's plea for clothing appropriate for the 'wet cold saisin' – overcoats, shoes, stockings and shirts – fell on deaf ears. Desertion by two Highland

companies – Menzies' and Balnagown's – soon reduced the strength to 900; sickness further weakened the garrison. And the heavy winter rains caused slippages in the earth ramparts. On 5 November, King William's birthday, the men from Grant's regiment nailed up the touch-holes of the guns pointing inland, but the arrival of money and provisions, together with a hanging or two, persuaded them to call off their mutiny.

Thereafter, the garrison settled down to its task of policing the western Highlands, and soldiers were out-posted to minor garrisons as far removed as Invergarry and Urquhart to the north, Tioram to the west, Duart to the south and Ruthven to the east. The men from Fort William, though, will always be remembered for their part in the appalling massacre at Glencoe in the early hours of 13 February, 1692. As Viscount Livingston, a leading perpetrator of the deed, wrote to the fort's deputy-governor shortly before that fateful day, it was 'a fair occasion...to show that your garrison serves for some use'. Some use! By the time the wintry sun broke over the glen, 38 men, women and children of the small clan of the

MacIains or MacDonalds that dwelt in the glen lay dead, either butchered by the redcoats or frozen in the heavy winter snows. Glencoe became known as the 'Glen of Weeping'.

Despite this terrible episode, gradually the garrison at Fort William began to assume an air of permanency. Shortly after the fort was finished, Governor Hill had received a royal charter for the creation of a town to be called Maryburgh in honour of the Queen. Laid out on ground to the south of the fort, Maryburgh was there chiefly as a sutlery, furnishing the garrison with all its needs (**colour plate 3**). Fort William was rapidly becoming a centre for the western Highlands. But it would appear that another leading player in the politics of the day had other ideas.

24 *John Campbell of Glenorchy, first Earl of Breadalbane; by Sir John Medina.*

Campbell's kingdom – Kilchurn

Sir John Campbell of Glenorchy (**24**) was head of the main cadet branch of the family that dominated Argyllshire society. The Campbells had acquired their immense wealth and power in the fifteenth century during the long and turbulent dismemberment of the mighty MacDonald empire, and Campbell of Glenorchy, born about 1635 and created first Earl of Breadalbane in 1681, seems to have inherited all of the unscrupulous cunning of his ancestors; indeed, he was described by one contemporary as a 'Highland Czarr'. During the events surrounding the downfall of James and the arrival of William and Mary, Breadalbane used all his devious skills to play a very dangerous political game. To some he was William's 'man of business', to others he was 'a known enemy of their Majesty's service'. Breadalbane seems only to have had one intention – to make himself undisputed master in the west.

Breadalbane's principal residence was Kilchurn Castle (**25** and see **colour plate 1**), majestically situated at the northern end of Loch Awe. Built by his ancestor, Sir Colin Campbell, first Lord of Glenorchy, in the middle of the fifteenth century, and remodelled a century later, it was 'ane real stronghold', a formidable battlemented tower house surrounded by a strong walled enclosure, or barmkin, and 'invirond on tuo sids with deep rivers, and a ditch and trench befor it'. It was to this Highland fastness that Breadalbane retired in the spring of 1689, whilst the events surrounding the proclamation of William and Mary as joint sovereigns unfolded. The story was put about that he was suffering from a bad attack of gout and 'sitting with soar foot at the fyr side'. He was in fact secretly furthering his ambition.

Breadalbane had already, in the mid 1680s, floated the idea of raising a Highland militia to police the troublesome Highlands. His ten plaided companies were to be under a 'principal person', namely himself. His proposal fell

25 *Kilchurn Castle from the north. The regular fenestration on the right, which lit the 1690s barrack rooms, contrasts with the rather haphazard array of openings of the medieval castle.*

on deaf ears but this did not deter him from pursuing his goal, in which a central element seems to have been his determination to convert his castle at Kilchurn into a garrison fort sufficient to rival Mackay's new Fort William. What the visitor sees today along the north side of the courtyard at Kilchurn is probably the oldest surviving barrack block on the mainland of Britain.

The work was supervised by Breadalbane's Chamberlain of Lorn, Alexander Campbell of Barcaldine, and carried out by Andrew Christie, 'mason in Balloch' (that is, Taymouth in Perthshire, another of Breadalbane's castles). Work began late in 1690 and was carried on throughout much of that decade, despite the great financial worries that beset his lordship. During that time, Kilchurn was substantially remodelled to provide accommodation for three companies of soldiers with their officers – about 200 men. In 1693, the Earl might well have witnessed the great door-lintel bearing the arms and initials of himself and his second wife, Countess Mary Campbell, who had died in 1691, being hauled into place above his front door.

In the absence of detailed accounts it is impossible to tell quite how the refurbished accommodation was to be used, in particular, the use now to be made of the tower house. It seems highly likely that it was no longer intended to serve as Breadalbane's private lodging but was downgraded to house the officer commanding the garrison. Similarly unclear is the use to which the south and west ranges in the courtyard were to be put, but a

role as quarters for senior officers seems most probable. Far more clear is the function for the new purpose-built L-shaped building along the north range (**26**). This block comprised three storeys of barrack rooms (accommodating a company on each floor) above a stone-vaulted basement incorporating two kitchens and associated service areas. Each floor in the main north block was clearly divided into four barrack rooms, and the floors in the north-east extension into two. Each room had a fireplace and at least two windows; latrines were provided at the junction of the two blocks. The slightly larger, and lighter, rooms in the north-east block, with their own kitchen in the basement, suggest that these served as quarters for the non-commissioned officers of the rank and file housed in the main north block. Additional accommodation was provided in the upper floors of the three projecting round towers now added to the medieval curtain wall and in the attic space.

This then was what Breadalbane was up to in those heady early days of the Williamite administration. It will forever remain a mystery quite what was in his mind for Kilchurn – and for Fort William for that matter – if he had ever got his way. Was Breadalbane simply building a safe house for himself? In which case it is very difficult to see how this squared with his determined efforts in the 1680s not to have a government garrison billeted on Kilchurn. Or was he seeing Kilchurn as a rival to Mackay's Fort William? In which case, why was he content simply to clothe Kilchurn in antiquated medieval defences – high walls and simple shot-holes – rather than in those 'state-of-the-art' bastioned defences? We shall never know. What we do know is that the last year for which significant building accounts for work on Kilchurn exist was 1698, the very year that work began on converting Fort

26 *Inside the shell of the barracks at Kilchurn Castle.*

William into a stone fort. The death knell had sounded on Campbell's kingdom.

James – King or Pretender?

The untimely death of Viscount Dundee and the ultimate failure of the first Jacobite Rising saw a measure of stability return to Scotland, Highlands and Lowlands alike, and the focus of military activity now shifted overseas, to Flanders. The reduction in the numbers of troops stationed in Scotland perforce led the Government to implement Breadalbane's main plan – the raising of independent companies of Highlanders as a militia force policing their own straths and glens. By and large they were reasonably successful.

On the political and constitutional fronts, matters were not so settled. Queen Mary had died in 1694 without bearing children and William was so grieved by her death that there seemed little likelihood of him marrying again and leaving an obvious heir. On the matter of the succession, therefore, speculation centred on Mary's younger sister, Anne, who had more than compensated for Mary's barrenness by producing 18 children. Tragically for her and for William's dynasty, none survived her, the last to die, William, Duke of Gloucester, passing away on 30 July 1700. Two years later, King William himself was dead, largely unmourned by his Scottish subjects, whom he had never deigned to visit, and by whom he stood accused of, at the least, indifference (the Massacre at Glencoe) and, at the worst, betrayal (the Darien disaster). He was succeeded by his sister-in-law, Anne, now aged 37 and most unlikely to bear another child. Who would succeed her? A rag-bag of claimants scattered throughout the royal houses of Europe, perhaps – of which the main contender was the House of Hanover (through Elizabeth of Bohemia, a daughter of James VI) – or the clear front-runner, James Francis Edward Stuart (**27**), the little child smuggled out of England with his parents, James VII and Mary

27 *James Francis Edward Stuart, the 'Old Pretender', contemplating an expedition to regain his lost throne; attributed to Francesco Trevisani.*

of Modena, in 1688. As far as the English were concerned, there was no contest – Hanover it was, anything to avert a Catholic succession. 'England would as soon have a Turk as a Roman Catholic for a King,' declared one Jacobite grandee. For the Scots, the matter was not so cut and dried for there was the strained relationship between the two countries to consider. The Act of Security, passed in 1704, even went as far as to declare that, in the event of Queen Anne's death, the Scots might opt for a monarch different from that succeeding to the English throne. As the temperature of the debate rose, so Jacobite hopes flickered into life once again. They were positively fanned into flames when the Act of Union between Scotland and England was passed in 1707.

The attempted Rising of the following year was made possible only with the support of King Louis XIV of France, partly because of his commitment to the Jacobite cause but perhaps also motivated by his determination to compensate for Marlborough's victories over the French at Blenheim, Ramillies and elsewhere, in which, incidentally, all six Scottish regiments fought with distinction. A fleet of 15 transports and five men-of-war were put at James's disposal. The Jacobites' promise to the French king, that 'the whole nation will rise upon the arrival of its king', in the event proved as worthless as the parchment it was written on. When a few of James's supporters travelling with him from Dunkirk stepped ashore at Pittenweem, in Fife, on 14 March 1708, they were met by just a handful of supporters. The appearance of the English Navy persuaded Admiral Forbin to abort the landing and the first attempt by King James VIII and III (if one was a Jacobite), or 'the Pretender' (as Queen Anne called her half-brother), to return to his birth-right was over.

The defence of 'North Britain'

The abortive Rising might have been over before it had begun, but that James Stuart had got so close to landing on Scottish soil and with such support from the French king alarmed Anne's London Government and prompted it into looking to the security of that part of the United Kingdom now prosaically called 'North Britain'. Given that the focus of the Rising had been on the east coast, so close to the heart of the old kingdom, the chief measures undertaken by the military authorities took place at the principal royal garrisons at Edinburgh and Stirling, but ever conscious of the cradle of Jacobite disaffection Fort William was included also.

Work began at all three places on 1 July

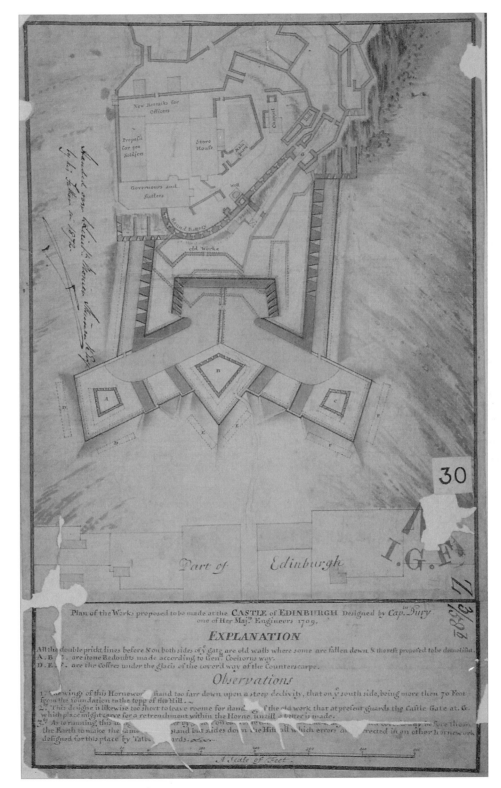

28 *Theodore Dury's plan for a new eastern defence at Edinburgh Castle.*

29 *Dury's Battery in Edinburgh Castle, and behind it the barracks designed to house officers and gunners serving in the garrison.*

1708, less than three months after James Stuart's return to France, and was directed by John Slezer's successor as engineer, Captain Theodore Dury. Dury had been in post at the Union and still served in that capacity, though he was now attached to the Board of Ordnance in London. The Board's roots were in the England of the Middle Ages and in Elizabeth I's time it had been created a Department of State responsible for armaments and military engineering, including the construction, upkeep and repair of defensive structures like castles and forts.

For Edinburgh Castle Dury proposed substantial changes to the perimeter defences (**28**). In the event his ambitious scheme for a great

30 *The caponier in the outer ditch at Stirling Castle.*

defence at the most vulnerable eastern front, mysteriously code-named *le grand secret*, was abandoned largely unfinished after grave doubts were raised about its effectiveness, and the odd wall below the present Esplanade is all that can be seen today. His plans for gun batteries covering the south and west sides – called Dury's Battery (**29**) and Butts Battery respectively – were completed, together with an upper battery on Hawk Hill, immediately west of Foog's Gate. (This was later abandoned and overwhelmed by the gargantuan New Barracks of the 1790s.) Dury also sought to upgrade significantly the barrack accommodation but succeeded only in having a new officers' block built on the west side of Palace Yard (the present-day Crown Square). Now called the Queen Anne Building, the two-storeyed structure housed some of the garrison officers, the castle gunners, the chaplain and others (**29**).

Dury proposed much the same ambitious programme for Stirling Castle (see **10**), and met with the same criticism of his planned forework

as he had at Edinburgh. This, too, had to be drastically altered during the course of construction work. However, much of what visitors see today as they approach the castle across the Esplanade and wend their way through the Outer Defences, is Dury's handiwork.

The work comprised a thick frontal wall housing the outer entrance gate and protected by a deep outer ditch. The wall was covered by sweeping fire from the sixteenth-century French Spur on the north side, now modified to house two tiers of guns, and from two caponiers (firing galleries) in the ditch (**30**). The northern part of the frontal wall formed part of a mighty bastioned artillery defence, now known as the Queen Anne Battery, that faced partly outwards to the field and partly inwards to cover an enclosed area between the outer and inner gates, now called Guardroom Square. It was hoped that any attackers getting thus far would be at the mercy of the enveloping fire-power. The inner gate gave access through the battery to the castle proper. The space beneath the terreplein, the broad level fighting platform behind the parapet of the massively thick battery, was put to additional use to accommodate a range of casemated rooms (**31**). In peace-time, these were for storing provisions, but during siege they were to be given over to the garrison to be used as temporary living quarters. Their usual buildings would be vulnerable to mortar attack but the stone-vaulted casemates, further covered by earth, were expected to withstand a direct hit. Each casemate was intended to hold up to 40 men. Dury's plans for upgrading the garrison buildings apparently came to nothing. These included the division of James IV's capacious Great Hall into a smaller banqueting room and garrison chapel and the insertion of floors, staircases and partitions into the adjacent Chapel Royal for barrack accommodation.

Fort William, too, received fresh attention following the 1708 emergency. Work had earlier been completed on facing the earthen ramparts and bastions in stone; now the impetus was given to transforming the garrison buildings, hitherto built of deals, into

31 *The row of stone-vaulted casemates beneath the terreplein of the Queen Anne Battery in Stirling Castle.*

stone also. Dury gave priority to a new powder magazine, situated within its own enclosure in the one full bastion at the south-east corner; to the governor's house, located at the far side of the fort beside the loch and housing also apartments for the lieutenant-governor, master gunner and storekeeper; and to two barrack buildings at the north-west corner of the enclosure. In 1711, plans were drawn up for the demolition of those buildings along the west side – two 'barracks of deals' and two houses for officers – and their replacement by one long barrack pile 'about 200 feet long [and giving] room for 9 chambers on one side, and as many on the other, is 18 Chambers the first story and 18 above maketh 36 in all, and reckoning 12 men in each room, this row will lodge 432 men'. A replacement provisions storehouse beside the governor's house and a new guardhouse beside the main gate followed over the next two years (**32**).

This great spurt of activity was concluded by the time Queen Anne died on 1 August 1714. Her successor, George Ludwig, Elector of Hanover, arrived in London in September to become George I and his accession proved the

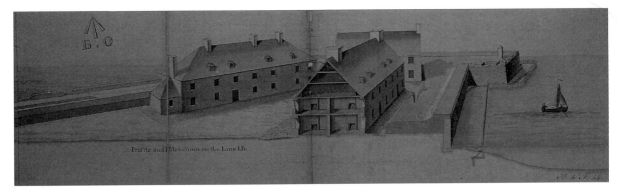

Profile and Elevations on the Line LL.

32 *A Board of Ordnance drawing of part of Fort William, dated 1733, and showing the governor's house (left), the storehouse (at the rear) and part of the soldiers' barracks built in the 1710s. The demi-bastion beyond the buildings is all that survives of Fort William today.*

spark to fan those Jacobite embers into life once more. Whisper of another Rising had already gripped the British Government before Anne's death; now the rumour spread like wildfire.

When the good folk of Inverness drowned out the official cry of 'God save the King' with their own shout of 'God damn them and their King' as the proclamation of his accession was read at the mercat cross, the Hanoverian administration knew it had problems. The garrison in Edinburgh Castle, in anticipation of trouble, had already dismantled the bridge, erected a drawbridge and dug a large trench around the side facing the town. Their precautions were to prove entirely warranted.

CHAPTER FOUR

The House of Hanover and the House of Stuart

There's some say that we wan,
Some say that they wan,
Some say that none wan at a', man;

But one thing I'm sure,
That at Sheriffmuir
A battle there was which I saw, man.
And we ran, and they ran and they ran and
we ran,
And we ran and they ran awa, man.

(Contemporary ballad recording the
Battle of Sheriffmuir, 1715)

The 1715 Rising

The popular contemporary ballad quoted above sums up the astonishing failure of the 1715 Jacobite Rising. The 1707 Treaty of Union had proved the greatest recruiting sergeant that the Jacobite cause could ever have wished for. The economic disappointment in Scotland, combined with the staggering, but perhaps understandable, political disregard for the Scots at Westminster throughout Queen Anne's reign, betrayed political ineptitude and miscalculation on an epic scale; Queen Anne herself spoke of the Scots as a 'strange people'. By 1714 the Scots, or at least the Highland clans, were openly discussing the accession of James VIII. Even in Westminster Tory Jacobites were easily appointed into Viscount Bolingbroke's administration. Jacobitism, of course, was not a phenomenon exclusive to Scotland, though it has with the passing of

time come to be seen as that. There were many in England and Wales who would have preferred a Stuart on the throne, although that support was perhaps more elusive when 'push came to shove', and it seems all the more surprising that George, Elector of Hanover was crowned with little initial opposition. As

33 *John Erskine, sixth Earl of Mar, with Stirling Castle in the background; by Sir Godfrey Kneller.*

Bolingbroke wrote afterwards, the 'thunder had long grumbled in the air; and yet when the bolt fell, most of our party appeared as much surprised as if they had no reason to expect it.'

When the opposition came it was orchestrated neither by Bolingbroke's ineffective moves in London nor from the Highlands, but entirely because of the chagrin of John Erskine, Earl of Mar (33). Despite attempting to ingratiate himself with the new king by penning a ludicriously sycophantic *Address* to him, Mar was summarily dismissed from the monarch's service. Only then did he remember his innate, deep-seated attachment to the 'king over the water'. It was Mar's duplicity and ineffective leadership, combined with the delayed appearance of James in 1715, that led to the failure of perhaps the best chance the Jacobite cause was ever to have.

By 1715 there was no real army in North Britain. The fortifications too had been starved of funds and none was in a defensible state, as Mar, an ex-Secretary of State, knew only too well. The two regiments, Hill's and Hamilton's, nominally stationed at Fort William, were reduced by disease to 340 effective men and scattered about the various outposts – 48 men on Mull to keep an eye on the MacLeans, others at the castles of Eilean Donan and Invergarry to watch the Mackenzies and the MacDonalds respectively. Nor could they hope for reinforcements since Ireland was mopping up every available man.

From the moment Mar left his ancestral seat of Kildrummy Castle in September 1715 to raise James Stuart's standard on the Braes of Mar there was widespread support. It came from the traditional lands in the north and east of Scotland, from men like the Earl Marischal and his kin, and from the Highland clans, the Camerons, the MacDonalds and the MacLeans. Some families were divided in their loyalties, like the MacGregors and the Murrays of Atholl; the Mackenzies, under the Earl of Seaforth, were initially rather half-hearted in their support, as was the Marquis

34 *The Jacobites attempt to take Edinburgh Castle in 1715; from a contemporary broadsheet.*

of Huntly. In the north of England, the Earl of Derwentwater brought out the Jacobite support and entrusted the command to Thomas Foster MP, who proved in the event as incompetent a leader as Mar.

One of Mar's prime objectives was to take Edinburgh Castle for the Pretender (34), and two days after the standard was raised the attempt was made by Lord Drummond, MacGregor of Balhaldy and Charles Forbes of Brux. It stands as an isolated incident within the Rising, but one that had repercussions in the minds of the fortress builders a decade later. The plot was simple. Two of the castle guards, James Thompson and John Holland, were bribed by Ensign Arthur and Sergeant

Ainslie into allowing a ladder to be thrown over the wall, by which a small force would climb and enter the castle, overcome the garrison and take the fortress. Even though the wife of Ensign Arthur had discovered the plot and informed Colonel Stewart, the deputy governor of the castle, the escapade might still have succeeded since Stewart failed to take the threat seriously and only slightly increased the guard. Lord Drummond with fifty High-landers picked from his estates in Perthshire and fifty more from Edinburgh waited below the crags at the Western Defences while Holland and Thompson were above waiting to pull up the ladders. Unfortunately Forbes had an important part of the ladder and was late appearing. Drummond decided to make the attempt without Forbes's section, which was a mistake as the ladder was too short. To round off a disastrous night, the officer of the day decided to make his rounds at 11.30 p.m., earlier than usual. The treacherous guards tried to save their necks by throwing down the ropes and firing on the party below, and the

35 *John Campbell, Second Duke of Argyll; by William Aikman.*

raiders scattered, meeting Forbes as they ran along the Nor' Loch (where Princes Street Gardens now is). The castle guard was not so lucky. Thompson and Holland escaped with a flogging but Ainslie was 'hanged by the neck in a reid coat over the castle wall near the postern gate'. The incident was over but the inherent weakness of the Western Defences and its postern gate was noted.

Whig support for the House of Hanover was strong in some parts of Scotland, with the Campbell Duke of Argyll (35) at its head. He was despatched to raise what forces he could to oppose the Rising. This amounted to 3300 regular soldiers, with a willing but almost useless Lowland militia in support – less than 4000 men all told. When the two armies finally met just outside Dunblane on 13 November 1715 Mar had more than twice that number of men, but he chose the occasion to demonstrate his incompetence as a soldier. The indecisive Battle of Sheriffmuir (36) that followed was fought just as the Rising in the north of England was being crushed in the aftermath of the Battle of Preston. The tide had turned, and Argyll breathed a sigh of relief for he had been convinced that his task was hopeless. He tried to convince the Government how lucky it had been and prayed that the 6000 soldiers being sent from Holland and the three regiments returning from Ireland would arrive before he needed to defend the House of Hanover again. He need not have worried for despite the arrival of a rather sulky James Stuart at Peterhead by Christmas the fight was all but lost. Argyll's long-awaited reinforcements arrived and advanced on Perth, which the Jacobites had captured in the first week of the Rising and heavily fortified with lines of 'entrenchments' (**colour plate 4**). But the Government army found no resistance, for James and his army had slunk away north-wards. The Jacobite cause received one final boost when £15,000 in Spanish gold was despatched from Calais in January 1716, but the Hanoverian good luck continued and the ship

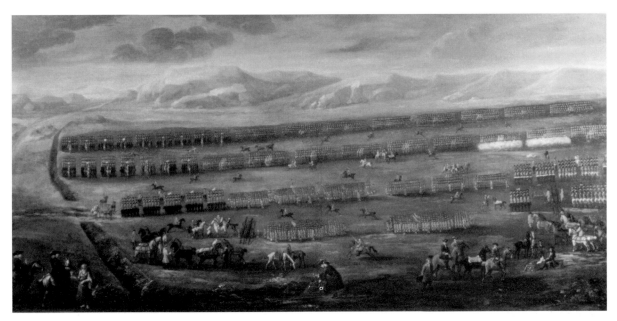

36 *The Battle of Sheriffmuir, 1715; by John Wootton.*

was wrecked on the sands of St Andrews' Bay in Fife. By 4 February, James was cashing in his return ticket to France – dejected and despairing. He was fated never to return to the land of his birth.

The outcome for the leaders of the Rising was predictable, at least for those who did not manage to escape with the Pretender and Mar to France. Those that did not lose their heads on the scaffold spent the next year or so hiding in the inaccessible corners of the Highlands or the Outer Isles, while their lands were declared forfeit; the mass of the Jacobite army evaporated into the hillside. A Disarming Act was passed and the army returned to its policing role. Their leader, Argyll, having 'thus gloriously finished the most laborious and hard campaign that was ever known, left the command of his Majesty's troops to Lieut-General Cadogan and in a day or two set out for London.' Cadogan thought that Argyll was too soft on the rebels, that he was prepared to offer 'very great civilities' to them, and with Argyll gone he was determined not to make the same mistake. Argyll, before departing,

had spread the army across Scotland. They were not only in the main garrisons of Edinburgh, Stirling, Fort William and Dumbarton, but in Glasgow, Fife, Perth, Dundee, Dunkeld, Montrose, Brechin, Aberdeen, Elgin and Inverness. It was in Inverness that Cadogan ensured that 'the Dutch [troops] have not left a chair or a stool, nor a barrell or a bottle, enfin nothing earthly undestroyed and the English troops very little more merciful.' But the molestation was short lived for the troops were needed elsewhere. Cadogan wished to be out of Scotland as quickly as he could and the soldiers were unhappy anywhere north of the Highland line.

A barracks for Berwick

Under the Disarming Act, the Jacobites had been compelled to surrender their arms, but worryingly for the Government 'as yett the number of arms got does not at all agree with the number that was in rebellion'. Despite this, a remarkable level of complacency still prevailed at Westminster. In 1716 the gunnery establishment was reorganised both to make savings and to make it more effective and, as the Duke of Marlborough was informed in

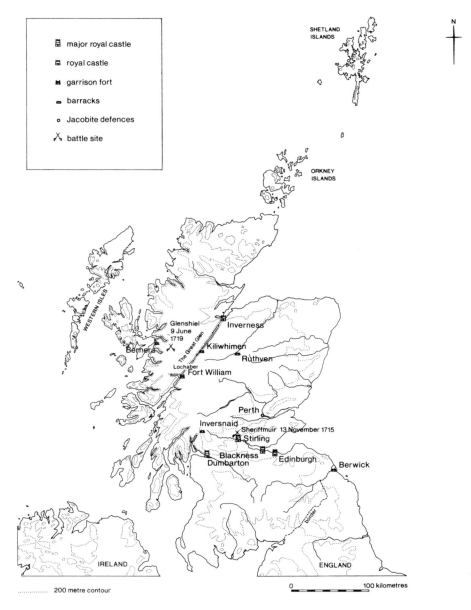

37 *The military places of strength 1715–24* (Chris Unwin).

July of that year, a 'saving [was] to be made on guns because in our several forts, castles, fortification and within our Kingdom of Great Britain [there] are much more than are necessary.' Here was an eighteenth-century Treasury-led 'options for change'. The guns in Edinburgh were reduced from 50 to 40, Stirling lost two; while Fort William astonishingly was reduced

from 68 to 30 and Berwick from 76 to 50.

Despite the fact that the main theatre of war during the 1715 Rising had been in the Scottish Lowlands, the main military development arising from it was a further attempt to gain a foothold in the unruly Highlands through a programme of barrack building (**37**). The exception was, surprisingly, an acknowledgement of the importance of Berwick as a staging post. Berwick, by now part of the North British army establishment along with

Hull and Carlisle, had long been an important post for armies moving north and south. It was a town which had suffered billeting for many years; there were times when the army more than doubled the population for months on end. The town fathers were frequently out of pocket. A dispute in 1679 over £3000 owed for quartering had still not been settled by 1705 when the first request for a proper barracks in the town was made. This was ignored and at the outbreak of the Rising in 1715 Captain Phillips, the Board of Ordnance engineer, had no time for such a notion, so busy was he demolishing houses immediately outside the town walls to improve the lines of sight for his gunners. But the Rising forced a rethink and it was agreed that the town should get its barracks, not to relieve the townsfolk of their 'irksome task' but to enable the free movement of troops; all the more important when the last of the Independent Highland

38 *Berwick Barracks from The Parade* (English Heritage).

Companies was disbanded in 1717 to be replaced by regular troops.

In 1717 the Board of Ordnance issued instructions for the building of a barracks for 36 officers and 600 men (**38**). It was to cost £4,937 10s 7d. A recent discovery of a preliminary sketch for the new barracks suggests that the architect was Nicholas Hawksmoor and not, as had previously been thought, his colleague Sir John Vanbrugh, whom Horace Walpole described as being less 'in the business of building houses so much as emptying quarries'. Both men were employed on occasions by the Board of Ordnance. Which ever of them was responsible, their connection with Berwick probably stopped at the design stage; nevertheless, they were responsible for one of the first purpose built, free-standing barracks designed for the Board of Ordnance in Britain (although there were already at least 80 places called barracks in Ireland).

The design was a rather severe military building with just enough Baroque flair to make it memorable. The engineer in charge of

the work was Captain Phillips, and for much of the time his work was overseen by Andrew Jelfe, an Essex architect who was the Board's surveyor and chief director in North Britain. Phillips was heavily involved in work at Hull also, but Berwick took up most of his time. He purchased stone, wood and slate as well as ordering 600,000 bricks from John Tully in Tweedmouth. Some of these bricks seem to have dropped off the back of a lorry on the way up Hide Hill to the barracks, for Phillips built himself a town house half way up!

The place as first built consisted simply of two piles of barracks facing each other across an open square, or parade ground. The northern gables of the piles were connected by a screen wall, which was punctuated centrally by the main gate, attractively decorated with the gilded arms of George I (**colour plate 5**). Immediately behind the screen wall was a guardhouse and small storehouse, the only buildings other than the barrack piles themselves.

Each pile comprised three stairs with four rooms off on each of the three floors (**39**). There was a further stair in the north end of each pile giving access to the officers' rooms in a pavilion stepped forward from the main façade. Each barrack room was designed to take eight men, an improvement on the twelve-to-a-room at Fort William of six years earlier. The men slept in four double cots and they were also provided with a table and two forms. The fireplace was used for cooking the food as well as heating the room, but then, as an Edinburgh landlady once remarked: 'It tak's a deal o' dirt to poison sogers.' There were no latrine blocks or washrooms, and the urine tub was 'slopped out' in the morning and fresh water put in for the coming night. Sleeping conditions, although no worse than in any billet, were cramped and unhealthy. One account graphically describes the men sleeping 'with all windows tightly shut, with the result that the atmosphere generally became so un-

39 *The east barrack pile at Berwick* (English Heritage).

40 *A smoke-drawing of Berwick Town Hall found in one of the barrack rooms at Berwick* (English Heritage).

bearable that the sergeant entering from the fresh morning was unable to bear the noisome atmosphere until windows were opened.' The officers' pavilions on the other hand offered a little more comfort and finesse, with slightly larger windows, more space and greater privacy (either single or at most double rooms) and subtly better architectural finishes.

The barracks were pretty well finished by 1720. However, the money was tight and, with insufficient funds to complete the fitting out of the barracks, the Board of Ordnance asked the town to pay the barrack master, John Sibbet, for the initial fitting out. Some time after Colonel Kirk's regiment first occupied the barracks Sibbet was requested to complete the bedding, since only one blanket per man had been supplied. Evidence from the building

itself also shows it was incomplete when first occupied. Some at least of the barrack rooms had not been plastered internally, and remained that way until after repairs in the late eighteenth century which included plastering the walls up to the newly placed ceiling. Above this later ceiling a series of smoke drawings (**40**) on plastered boards between the joists of the floor above was discovered recently. In February 1721, Sibbet was appointed for 21 years to 'repair and furnish the beds and complete in ye utensils belonging to ye barracks at Berwick' for £70 a year. An additional £10 was voted to him for the keeping of the barracks on Holy Island, and Tynemouth Barracks was also being repaired and fitted out for occupation at the same time.

Berwick Barracks very soon became too small. This was through no fault of Hawks-moor's for there was then no tradition of bar-rack building to inspire him. By 1740 another pile, the Clock Block, was being built along

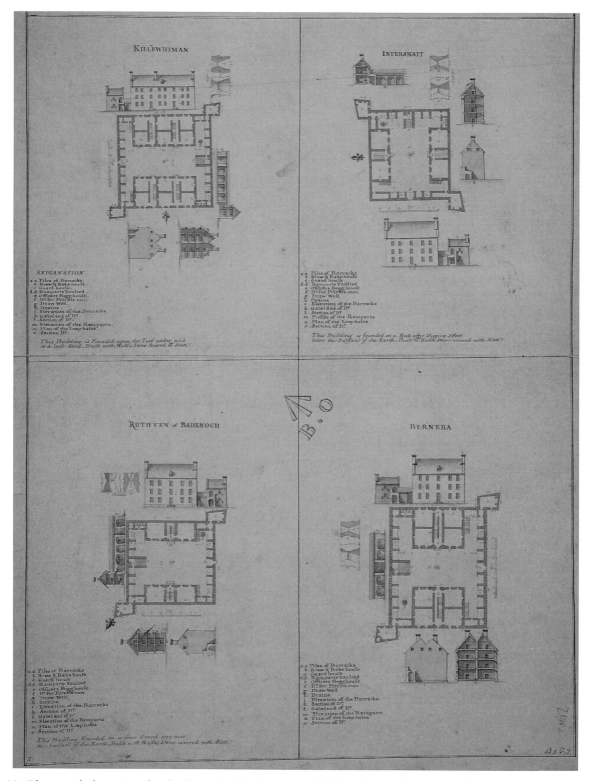

41 *Plans and elevations by the Board of Ordnance of all four barracks proposed to be built in the Highlands in the aftermath of the 1715 Rising.*

the south side opposite the main gate, whilst a nearby private house was pressed into service as a hospital.

Highland barracks

In April 1718, Patrick Strachan of Glenkindie was seeking payment for his attendance from 20 November 1717 to 20 February 1718 when he 'came from the Highlands by order of the Lord Justice Clerk, to give in schemes of the most proper places for building barracks' in the Highlands. It had been decided in August 1717 that new barracks would be built there. They were to support the existing garrisons and be sited at important cross-roads. Andrew Jelfe's predecessor as surveyor to the Board, James Smith, surveyed several sites with a view to building barracks, including Dalnacardoch, Garvamore, Lochlogan, Glenshishie and Glen Moriston. In the event, four locations were agreed on – Bernera, Inversnaid, Kiliwhimen and Ruthven in Badenoch – and Smith proceeded to draw up detailed plans (41).

Inversnaid (42) was built in the shadow of Ben Lomond on land forfeited by Rob Roy MacGregor. The site was chosen more to repay MacGregor and his clan for the irritation they had caused to the Government and to the Duke of Montrose's rent collectors than

42 *The Hanoverian legacy lives on at Inversnaid in the modern farm name even though precious little survives of the eighteenth-century barracks.*

to protect the strategic line from Dumbarton to Atholl. Bernera was built on MacLeod land in Glenelg to cover the short sea crossing across the Sound of Sleat to the Isle of Skye (**colour plate 6**). Kiliwhimen (or Kilcumein) was built on Fraser land at a strategic point mid-way along the Great Glen; it was later replaced by Fort Augustus. Lastly, Ruthven in Badenoch (**43** and **front cover**) was built in the Spey valley on land owned by the Duke of Gordon, on the site of a medieval castle that had served as a garrison post as late as 1689.

The construction of the four barracks progressed very slowly; this was an army of occupation which had always to watch its back, as the eight masons and quarriers snatched by armed Highlanders from Inversnaid in August 1718 would have testified to, had they ever been returned! The first essential was the building of a small guarded encampment for the workmen and soldiers. The records for the supply of equipment to a detachment from Brigadier Wightman's regiment attending the works at Inversnaid make it clear that they were expected to provide everything from bedding to the officers' damask table cloths.

The construction works were supervised by James Smith and his immediate successors. Smith, who had been overseer of the royal works in Scotland in the time of Charles II, was now rather elderly for the task and in January 1719, at the age of 70, he was dismissed from his post as 'surveyor and chief director for carrying on the barracks in North Britain' for not using 'the necessary dispatch' in the building of the four barracks – hardly a fitting end to a fine career. He was replaced by Andrew Jelfe, newly arrived from Berwick. Although a man with considerable experience, Jelfe found working in Scotland trying, and working with Patrick Strachan of Glenkindie even more exasperating. By 1720 he had been replaced by Captain John Romer, who was to be one of the Board's finest military engineers and who left a considerable legacy in Scotland. These three men were supported by

43 *Ruthven Barracks.*

draughtsmen, engineers and overseers who moved between the sites as each proceeded. Regularly recurring names are Lieutenants Bastide and Dumaresq, Major Gordon and Robert Douglas.

The first two barracks to be built were those at Inversnaid and Kiliwhimen, and apart from the snatching of the eight men at Inversnaid everything went reasonably well. By way of contrast the history of the building of Bernera and Ruthven verges at times on comic farce. Sir Patrick Strachan had agreed in January 1719 to produce the two sets of barracks with all speed, and then proceeded to prevaricate. Months turned into years. The 1719 Rising, played out within ten miles of the proposed site of Bernera, came and went – and still no barracks appeared. Strachan agreed to complete them by 1720, but since the ground at Glenelg was not broken until May of that year the Board of Ordnance had every right to doubt him. Nonetheless, by 1722 Strachan had been given a warrant as barrack-master general for North Britain. In the event, Bernera was completed only in April 1723 and Ruthven, though occupied before Bernera, did

not receive its finishing touches until 1724.

The craftsmen working on the first two barracks, Inversnaid and Kiliwhimen, were the usual Board of Ordnance labour force. Robert Mowbray, master carpenter, can be found working from Berwick to Fort William, as can master mason Gilbert Smith, who was James Smith's son-in-law, James Syme, slater, and George and John Ryalton, bricklayers. However, only Mowbray's name is found in connection with the building of Bernera and Ruthven, suggesting that Strachan was able to employ his own team.

Smith's design for the four barracks was standard, although no two are exactly alike (**44**). They each had two piles of barracks facing each other across a barrack square, as at Berwick. The rear of both piles formed part of the enclosing wall. This wall was designed to resist an assault by lightly-armed Highlanders but not to withstand a siege with artillery. The wall was furnished with vaulted musket-looped positions open to the rear and with a walkway over (**45**). The four corners of each barracks were to have angled corner towers 'if ye money answers', giving the barracks at least the appearance of providing enfilading fire along the walls. The money

44 *Reconstruction of Ruthven Barracks under siege in 1745 (Dave Pollock).*

45 *A stretch of musket-looped wall behind the Lovat Arms Hotel, Fort Augustus, is all that survives of Kiliwhimen Barracks.*

46 *The north barrack pile at Bernera, built to accommodate two companies of soldiers (about 120 men).*

clearly did not answer for in the event only two towers were built at opposing corners. These towers also had domestic functions, as guardrooms, bakehouse and brewhouse at ground level, and as officers' quarters on the floor above.

The size of the garrisons varied according to the number of men to be provided for. Kiliwhimen was to be the biggest, housing six companies, or about 360 men. (Since 1700 a company of foot had been regularised at 60 men per company in wartime and 40 in peacetime.) Second in size came Bernera with four companies (240 men), with Ruthven and Inversnaid each holding two companies (120 men). The barrack piles were all three-storeyed with basements and attics providing accom-

modation for stores. Inversnaid and Ruthven were single-pile, with just two rooms on each of the three floors while Bernera kept the same five-bay façade but doubled the number of rooms per floor by using a double-piled construction, so creating the M-shaped gable (**46**). Kiliwhimen was also double-piled but had an additional stair giving an eight-bay façade.

The rooms were almost square, measuring just under 5.5m (18ft). Each had a fireplace and five double beds 'in as little room as can well be allowed'. As at Berwick there were no communal messing or kitchen facilities, and the barrack rooms had to serve as sleeping, cooking, eating and living rooms. The Highland barracks, however, did have one extra facility over Berwick; separate latrines, one for officers and one for the rank and file, were provided beside the barrack piles. Robert Mowbray was paid for delivering the furnishings for Inversnaid in June 1721 – 50

1 *Kilchurn Castle and Loch Awe, Argyll.*

2 *An undated bird's-eye view of Edinburgh Castle by John Slezer. Whilst his depiction of the buildings is accurate, the great bastioned forework was a figment of his imagination and, sadly, never built.*

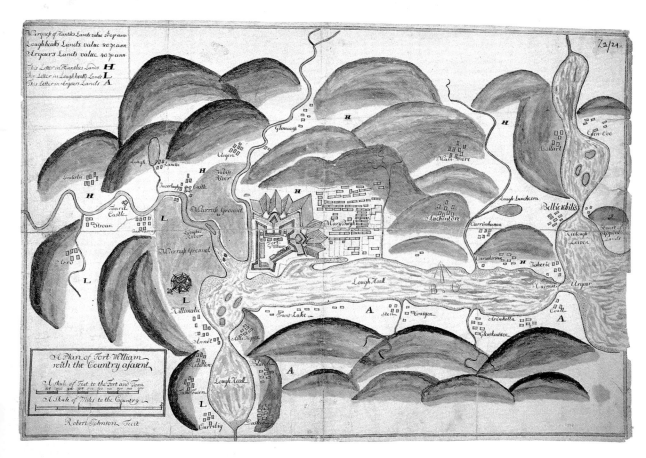

A Marquess of Huntlies Lands value 70 p ann
Loughheals Lands value 80 p ann
Urquarts Lands value 40 p ann

This Letter in Huntlies Lands   **H**
This Letter in Loughheals Lands   **L**
This Letter in Urquars Lands   **A**

A Plan of Fort William
with the Country adjasent

A Scale of Feet to the Fort and Town

A Scale of Miles to the Country

Robert Johnson Fecit

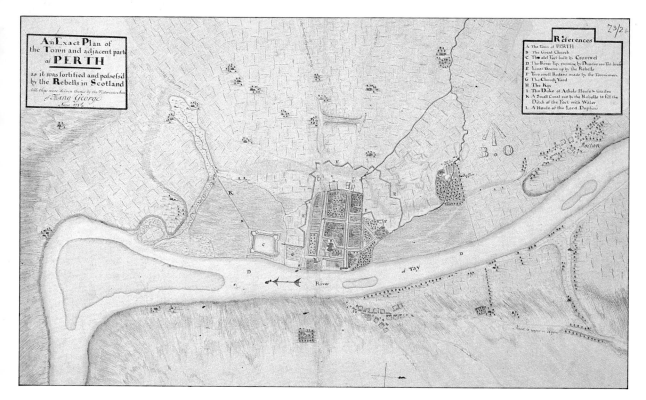

An Exact Plan of
the Town and adjacent parts
of PERTH
as it was fortified and possess'd
by the Rebells in Scotland
till they were driven thence by the Victorious Arms
of King George
June 1716

References

A The Town of PERTH
B The Great Church
C The old Fort built by Cromwel
D The River Tay running by Dundee see Patricia
E Lines thrown up by the Rebells
F Two small Redans made by the Townesmen
G The Church Yard
H The Kay
I The Duke of Athole House & Garden
K A Small Canal cut by the Rebells to fill the
   Ditch of the Fort with Water
L A House of the Lord Duplin

3 'A plan of Fort William with the country adjacent'; drawn by Robert Johnson for the Board of Ordnance about 1720. By this date, Mackay's 1690 scheme had come to fruition.

4 A drawing by the Board of Ordnance of Perth as it was fortified by the Jacobites during the 1715 Rising. The Cromwellian citadel is still clearly visible.

5 The arms of King George I above the gateway into Berwick Barracks. The arms are quartered: 1 England and Scotland; 2 France; 3 Ireland; 4 Hanover (with its white horse and the golden crown of Charlemagne) (English Heritage).

6 Bernera Barracks, Glenelg, and the Sound of Sleat; by John Bastide.

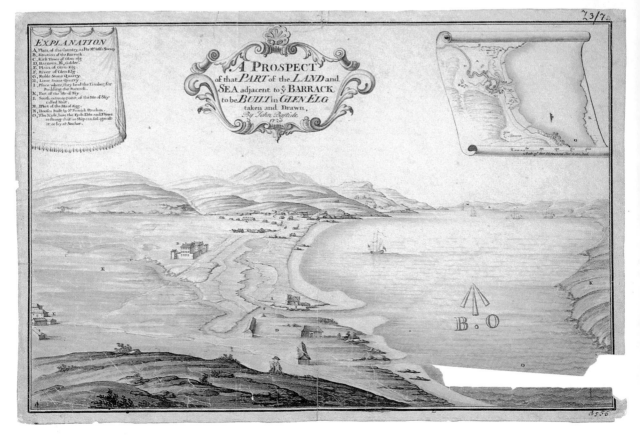

7 *Field-Marshall George Wade; attributed to Johan van Diest. In the background is a working party creating one of his cherished military roads, probably that crossing over the Corrieyairack Pass between Ruthven Barracks and Fort Augustus.*

8 *A Board of Ordnance plan of Fort Augustus, dated 1734, showing the new fort and the nearby Kiliwhimen barracks.*

9 *Edinburgh Castle from the north west. The zigzag fortifications skirting the crest of the crags date from the 1730s while the buildings looming up behind are largely later-eighteenth century in origin.*

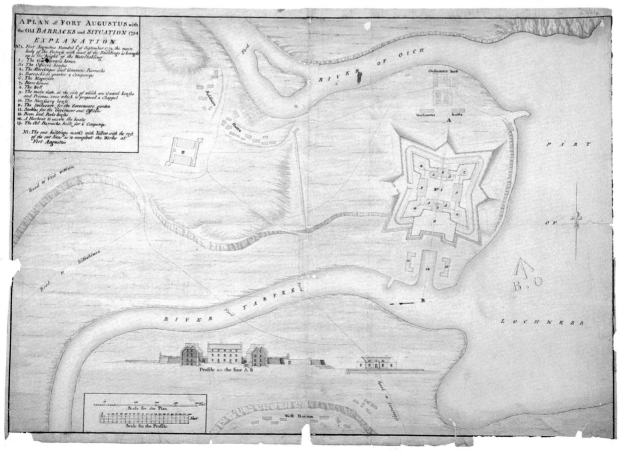

10 *The Battle of Culloden,*
16 April 1746; by Thomas
Sandby.

11 *Fort George Ardersier,*
looking westward across the
Moray Firth towards
Chanonry Point, the Black
Isle and the mountains of
northern Inverness-shire.

12 *The parade at Fort George*
with the artillery and staff
blocks beyond. The
pavilions at either end
provided houses for the
Governor (left), lieutenant-
governor and fort-major
(right).

13 *Paul Sandby's depictions of*
the castles of Tioram and
Duart, drawn in 1748.

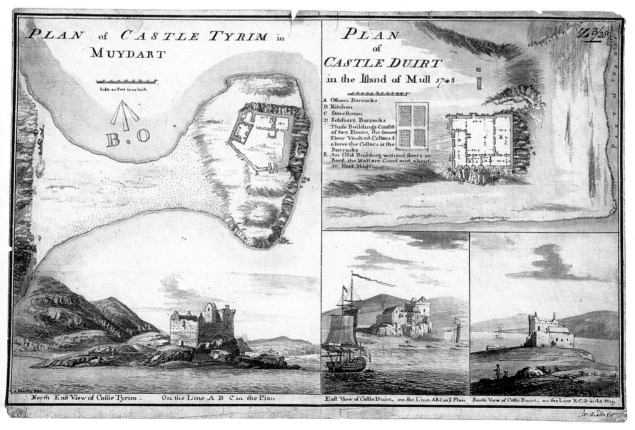

PLAN of CASTLE TYRIM in MUYDART

Scale 40 Feet to an Inch

B. O

PLAN of CASTLE DUIRT in the Island of Mull 1748

A Officers Barracks
B Kitchen
C StoreRoom
D Soldiers Barracks
  Those Buildings Consist
  of two Floors, the Ground
  Floor Vaulted Cellars &
  above the Cellars is the
  Barracks
E An Old Building without floors or
  Roof, the Wall are Good and about
  50 Feet High

North East View of Castle Tyrim.   On the Line A.B.C in the Plan

East View of Castle Duirt, on the Line A.B.C in y Plan   South View of Castle Duirt, on the Line E.C.D in the Plan

14 *Corgarff Castle, in Strathdon, a medieval tower house requisitioned by the military in 1748 and converted into a barracks for a company of soldiers charged with policing this remote and lawless region.*

15 *Three soldiers of the British Army, painted by David Morier about 1750 for the Duke of Cumberland. The Invalids Regiment manned many of the Highland forts and barracks in the later eighteenth century; the 42nd Regiment of Foot later became known as The Black Watch.*

bedsteads at 15s each, 12 tables at 11s and 24 forms at 7s. He supplied the same for Ruthven in September of that year. For Kiliwhimen he supplied 75 beds, 18 tables and 36 benches. From this it is clear that the projected numbers of men for each barracks was destined not to be achieved immediately. Each bed required a flock bed, a bolster, three coverlets and three Witney blankets, the whole costing £4 4s per bed. Barrack fittings were paid for by the barrack master appointed to the keeping of the barracks. From 1722 this was none other than Strachan himself who was given £200 a year to cover all four. In addition, he was by 'virtue of his commission being obliged to provide fire and candles at all the barracks to such of the troops as are quartered there at a certain allowance for each man according to the direction of the Commander-in-Chief for North Britain.' A hint of the siege mentality comes out in the same document: 'your memorial did contract with proper persons at Fort William for cutting of turf for the garrison at Bernera, and the contraction went from Fort William, which is 40 miles distant and carried servants with him for that effect. But to the great surprise of the memorialist one Ensign Johnston of Colonel Kirk's regiment who commanded at Bernera at that time, being 24th April past [1722], would not allow the cutting of any turf even in the map that lies within the limits marked out for the King for the use of the barracks, nor could he show any order for so doing.'

A supply of water was essential. The original plans for all four garrisons indicate a well within each enclosure. At Kiliwhimen there was clearly a problem with the supply and an elaborate water-collection system was proposed. It gathered the water from the roofs and transported it to underground cisterns beneath the parade ground. The well visible today at Ruthven is in neither of the two positions indicated on Smith's building plans, and recent excavation has shown that the present well was that which had served the medieval castle and which was probably encountered during construction work and brought back into service.

Another significant alteration to the original design was the addition of musket loops in the outer walls of the barrack blocks (though these were subsequently blocked up again at Ruthven). Most notably, the plan of Bernera as drawn was reversed on the ground, and someone seems to have held the plan upside down since there is no apparent topographical reason for the change. Bernera was the last to be built and Sir Patrick clearly felt he had time to add a few architectural flourishes to the basic design. The openings in the barracks were given segmental-arched heads, there were dressed freestone plinths and detailing on the chimney-stacks and gables, and the main entrance was through a decorated arched opening (see **46**).

Although the four barracks continued to be occupied throughout much of the eighteenth century their inadequacy was recognised very early on by Major-General Wade, who pointed out the inherent defensive weaknesses of two of the four garrisons because of their topographical situation (presumably Inversnaid and Kiliwhimen). More damning still, he wrote, 'It is to be wished that during the Reign of Your Majesty and Your Successors, no Insurrections may ever happen to experience whether the Barracks will effectually answer the end proposed.'

The 1719 Rising

An uneasy peace returned to the Highlands after the 1715 Rising. The forfeiture of estates had proved more of a bother than a blessing and the erstwhile Jacobite leaders were allowed to come out of hiding and take up the tenor of their lives once more. But this strange calm was soon interrupted. A whiff of further trouble came in 1717 when a Swedish-backed plot to advance the Pretender's cause was discovered by a 44-year-old major-general in the king's army named George Wade, though it is not clear how serious the Swedes were beyond their willingness to take Jacobite money. And then in 1719 came one of the most bizarre episodes in the history of Jacobite disaffection. This time the driving force was neither France nor Sweden but Spain and its involvement was entirely a political device to raise the profile of that country's first minister, Cardinal Alberoni, an Italian gardener's son. In 1718 the Spanish fleet had been soundly beaten by the British Navy at Cape Passaro and Alberoni was not amused. Intent on revenge he considered that the easiest way to achieve this was to support another Jacobite Rising. The plot was hatched: the main force commanded by the Duke of Ormonde was to attack the south-west of

England, whilst George Keith, the Earl Marischal of Scotland, was to lead a diversionary attack on the western Highlands.

The plan got off to a wretched start when Ormonde's huge invasion fleet encountered a violent storm off Cape Finisterre in March 1719 and was scattered to the four winds. Blissfully ignorant of this news, the Earl Marischal with the Marquis of Tullibardine, another Jacobite stalwart, and a force of 307 Spanish infantrymen sailed from France and reached Stornoway where they were joined by a second small force led by the Earl Marischal's brother, James Keith. Almost as soon as they had dropped anchor they squabbled and the time not spent arguing was spent in reaching out for support from the traditional Jacobite heartlands. This proved elusive, the Lowland Jacobites in particular refusing to make any show of public support until the Duke of Ormonde had successfully landed. Still

47 Eilean Donan Castle, on Loch Duich. The present-day castle and bridge largely date to the restoration of 1912.

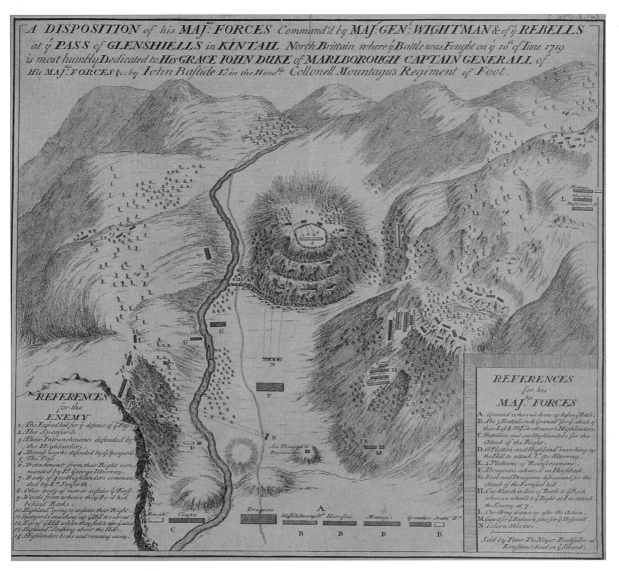

A DISPOSITION of his MAJ: FORCES Command'd by MAJ: GEN: WIGHTMAN & of y REBELLS at y PASS of GLENSHIELLS in KINTAIL North Brittain where y Battle was Fought on y 10th of June 1719 is most humbly Dedicated to His GRACE JOHN DUKE of MARLBOROUGH CAPTAIN GENERALL of His MAJ: FORCES &c: by John Bastide Lt in the Honoble Collonell Mountagus Regiment of Foot.

48 *The Board of Ordnance's drawing of the Battle of Glenshiel, 1719; by John Bastide.*

bickering, they moved to the mainland and established their base at the old Mackenzie stronghold of Eilean Donan (47). The Earl Marischal was for marching on Inverness; Tullibardine was for staying put. Then came the news of Ormonde's disaster at sea, but before they could effect their escape, the British Navy had blocked their seaward exit and General Wightman's army, marching from Inverness, was fast approaching from the east.

The Jacobites and Spaniards, numbering 'not above a thousand men', had no option but to stand and fight. When the two small armies met in the Pass of Glenshiel (48), not ten miles from the building site that was to be Bernera Barracks, on 9 June 1719 they were evenly matched. The battle lasted much of the day, with about a hundred killed or wounded on each side. By evening the Jacobite army was routed and on the following morning the Spaniards, probably wondering quite what they were doing there at all, surrendered. The Jacobite leaders all escaped, and their army once again

67

evaporated into the hillside leaving the Spanish to be herded off to Edinburgh to await their fate. In the event they were shipped back to Spain – at Spanish expense!

This farcical episode reinforced in the minds of the Hanoverian Government, for the moment at least, the need to keep a watch in the western Highlands as well as the importance of completing the four barracks, one of which, Bernera, could have served it well in this episode had it been completed in time. But the failure of the '15 and the '19 saw the Jacobite cause reach its lowest ebb and the Government was soon of a mind to do what it most wished – forget Scotland existed. That they were not able to do so was down to the crafty agitation of Simon Fraser of Lovat, the 'Spider of Dounie', and the studied response from the man who had exposed that Swedish plot back in 1717 – Major-General George Wade.

CHAPTER FIVE

An Irishman Abroad – Wade in Scotland

Had you seen these roads before they were made,
You would hold up your hands and bless General Wade.

(Attributed to Major William Caulfeild, Wade's baggage master and inspector of roads)

Wade's warrant

In the very year – 1690 – that General Mackay began the building of Fort William, a 17-year-old Anglo-Irishman called George Wade (**colour plate** 7) was gazetted ensign into the Earl of Bath's Regiment, the 10th Foot. His army career was set for a meteoric rise – lieutenant by 1693, captain-lieutenant by 1695, lieutenant-colonel by 1703, colonel by 1707, brigadier-general by 1708 and major-general shortly after the Elector of Hanover's accession in 1714. He had seen action in Flanders, Portugal and Spain. As major-general, his first taste of action was not against a foreign foe but the new king's disloyal subjects in Bath, a hotbed of Jacobitism. The manner in which he smoked out the plotters, and how in 1717 he further exposed 'a design to raise a rebellion in His Majesty's dominions, to be supported by a force from Sweden', obviously endeared him to his sovereign. And when a lengthy and highly disturbing account, or memorandum 'concerning the State of the Highlands', written by Simon Fraser, Lord Lovat, arrived on

George I's desk in 1724, it was to his trusted major-general that the king turned for help.

On 3 July 1724, Wade was instructed to proceed to Scotland with all haste. He was:

> narrowly to inspect the present situation of the Highlanders, their manners, customs, and the state of the country in regard to the depredations said to be committed in that part of his Majesty's dominions; to make strict enquiry into the allegations that the effect of the last Disarming Act had been to leave the loyal party in the Highlands naked and defenceless at the mercy of the disloyal; to report how far Lovat's memorandum was founded on fact, and whether his proposed remedies might properly be applied; and to suggest to the King such other remedies as may conduce to the quiet of his Majesty's faithful subjects and the good settlement of that part of the Kingdom.

Wade, evidently appreciating the urgency of the situation, set off for Scotland the following morning. By 10 December his full report was delivered to the king.

If Lovat's memorandum had caused the Hanoverian king to furrow his brow, then Wade's report must have brought him out in a cold sweat. Of 22,000 men in the Highlands capable of bearing arms, he began, '10,000 are well affected to the Government, the remainder have been engaged in Rebellion against Your Majesty, and are ready, whenever encouraged by their Superiors or Chiefs of

Clans, to create new Troubles and rise in Arms in favour of the Pretender.' That set the tenor for the rest of the report.

Wade concluded his assessment with a number of suggestions as to what might be done to address the appalling situation. Included among them were the following:

> That Companies of such Highlanders as are well affected to his Majesty's Government be Established, under proper Regulations and Commanded by Officers speaking the Language of the Country...[and] That the said Companies be employed in Disarming the Highlanders, preventing Depredations, bringing Criminals to Justice, and hinder Rebells and Attainted Persons from inhabiting that part of the Kingdom.

> That a Redoubte or Barrack be erected at Inverness, as well for preventing the Highlanders descending in the Low Country in time of Rebellion, as for the better Quartering of his Maty's Troops, and keeping them in a Body sufficient to prevent or Subdue Insurrections. That in order to render the Barrack at Killihuimen (Kiliwhimen) of more use than I conceive it to be of at present (from its being situate at too great a distance from Lake Ness) a Redoubte be built at the West End adjoining to it...

> That a small Vessel with Oars and Sails be built on the Lake Ness, sufficient to carry a Party of 60 or 80 Soldiers and Provisions for the garrison, which will be a Means to keep the Communication open between that place and Inverness, and be a safe and ready way of sending Parties to the Country bordering on the said lake, which is Navigable for the largest vessels.

The Government's response to Wade's alarming report was swift, reflecting the seriousness with which it viewed the situation, and by Christmas Day Wade was Commander-in-Chief of all His Majesty's forces, castles, forts and barracks in North Britain. In the following April, Wade submitted his first request for money – £10,000, to be spent over two years. Among the items on his shopping list were the embodiment of the Highland Companies, the vessel for Loch Ness, a new fort for Inverness, and major repairs to Edinburgh Castle and Fort William. Wade was clearly having second thoughts about upgrading the barracks at Kiliwhimen, considering instead the possibility of building an entirely new 'fort and barracks' (**49**).

The major-general's list included another item not in his original submission, that 'for mending the Roads between the garrisons and barracks, for the better Communication of his Majesty's Troops'. Of all Wade's achievements in the course of his fifteen years in Scotland, it was these roads which were to bring him enduring fame.

New roads through the glens

Wade supervised the building of some 250 miles (400km) of road and about 40 bridges. No matter that his assistant and successor as road-builder, Major William Caulfeild, was responsible for at least four times that length of road and 20 times that number of bridges – a legacy for which he has never received the recognition due to him – it was Wade himself who secured the initial Government approval, and the finance, for such a novel idea and established the framework of the system.

The importance of good roads to military efficiency had been impressed on Wade in 1708 when, as second-in-command to General Stanhope in Minorca, he had seen how 'a very good road' had enabled heavy siege guns to be transported across a hilly and rocky terrain, ground not dissimilar in fact to the Highlands of Scotland. In his initial report to King George, Wade gave an inkling of the direction his mind was going:

> Before I conclude this Report, I presume to observe to your Mat', the great Disadvantages Regular Troops are under when they engage with those who Inhabit Mountainous Situations. The Sevennes in France, the

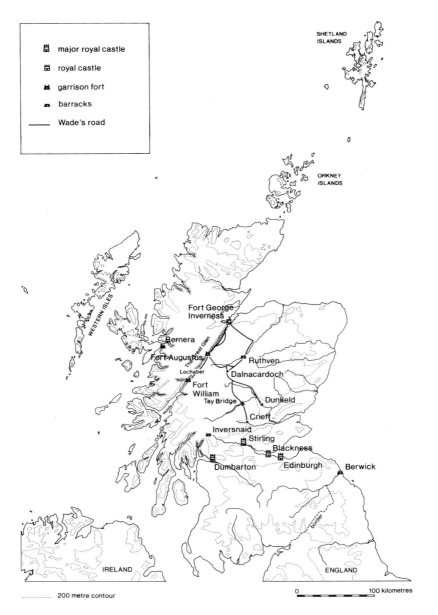

49 *The military places of strength and roads 1725-44 (Chris Unwin).*

Catalans in Spain, have in all times been Instances of this Truth. The Highlands of Scotland are still more impractible, from the want of Roads and Bridges, and from excessive Rains that almost continually fall in those parts, which by Nature and constant use become habitual to the Natives, but very difficultly supported by the Regular Troops.

There were already roads in existence of course – a Board of Ordnance map showing the road between Inversnaid and Fort William,

dated 1718, makes that perfectly clear (**50**) – and Wade's own use of the word 'mend' in his 1725 report confirms this. But his concern was that such roads scarcely deserved the name, so appalling were they. They might have been capable of carrying a modest amount of infantry, but they were emphatically no use for large movements of troops or for wheeled

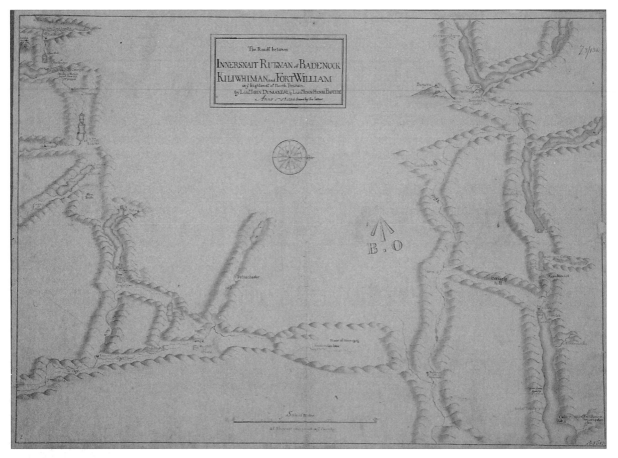

50 *A pre-Wade road map, dated 1718, charting the route between the barracks at Inversnaid, Ruthven and Kiliwhimen and the garrison at Fort William. Present-day motorists are advised not to rely too heavily on this map as they tour the Highlands!*

traffic, like baggage- and gun-trains.

Wade arrived in Scotland in mid June and work was soon underway on building a suitable road in the Great Glen to link Fort William with the barracks at Kiliwhimen. The *Edinburgh Evening Courant* for 7 November reported that the 'roads, hardly possible for a single man, are widened and mended for 9 miles'. Between then and 1736, the last year in Wade's tour of duty in which any expense is recorded for the road programme, four major routes were created: Fort William to Inver-

ness, Dunkeld to Inverness, Crieff to Dalnacardoch and Dalwhinnie to Fort Augustus.

Road planning and surveying was meticulously carried out, largely by Wade himself who travelled to Scotland each spring and remained for the high season. In Caulfeild's day, a typical survey party comprised an NCO and six soldiers – one to carry the theodolite, two to carry the measuring chain, one each for the fore and back stations, and one to act as batman (**51**). It was probably the same in Wade's time also. Care was taken in the siting of the roads. The Roman preference for driving a road in a straight line from one vantage point to another was generally preferred. Where steep gradients were encountered traverses, or hair-pins, were used, the most spectacular being those carrying the road over the Corrieyairack Pass between Ruthven

Barracks and Fort Augustus, built in 1731. Suitable crossing-places across burns and rivers were a controlling factor. Wade preferred to avoid the expense of bridge building if an obstacle could be forded at far less cost.

Wade's roads were constructed during the summer months, between 1 April and 31 October. The bulk of the work was carried out by the soldiers who were to use them, and about 500 men were employed on each road (52). Specialised work, like joinery and stone-masonry, was contracted out to civilians. At the start of each season, the working parties (Wade called them his 'Highwaymen') left their

51 *Paul Sandby's drawing of a survey party near Kinloch Rannoch, in Perthshire, showing the surveyor, his six assistants and their military escort.*

winter garrisons for the hills. Each party consisted of 1 captain, 2 subalterns, 2 sergeants, 2 corporals, 1 drummer and 100 men. Surprisingly, given the relatively high cost, soldiers engaged on the road-building programme were paid double-time. The catch was that for every day they weren't able to work because of the weather they got nothing at all!

The working parties generally lived in hutted camps about 10 miles apart; exceptionally they lived under canvas. Their tools – pick-axes, spades, crow-bars and such like – were brought from central stores whilst their rations – food, drink, fuel, even medicines – were provided by their captain, who was paid an extra 'two shillings and sixpence per diem [for] making the necessary provision for their tables from distant parts'. Apparently, this could include setting up camp breweries so as to prevent the men from

52 Workmen shifting boulders during road making; by Paul Sandby.

having to drink the unwholesome water or the strong spirits made by the locals. The excise was not amused but it could do little about it.

Wade seems to have laid down general ground rules for the construction of his roads and bridges. These included a standard width for the roads of about 5m (16ft), reducing to 3m (10ft) in difficult terrain, and a standard form of road-construction (a base of large boulders covered by smaller broken stones and topped with gravel). However, archaeological excavations on the Dunkeld – Inverness road

have suggested that adherence to the norm was not automatically followed. It seems that decisions were taken 'on the spot' to adjust the specification, depending on local factors, like the presence of an acceptable glacial till. With notable exceptions, like his cherished Tay Bridge at Aberfeldy (53), Wade's standard bridge was of plain rubble masonry, with straight, parallel spandrels and side walls, an overall width at the crown of no more than 4.2m (14ft), and a harled, or roughcast, finish (54).

Roads were not the only way of conveying troops and provisions around the Highlands, as Wade's shopping list made clear, and shortly after his arrival in the Highlands in 1725 work was in hand on building 'a pretty large vessel for transporting of Men, Provisions, Baggage, etc … upon the Lake Ness' The idea was nothing new; in 1655 Cromwell's troops had 'carried a bark driven upon rollers [from Inverlochy] to the lochend of Ness, and there enlarged it into a stately frigate to sail with provisions from one end of the loch to the other'. Wade's new 'galley', all 30 tons of her, capable of carrying up to 80 men and armed with up to eight guns, was almost his undoing. In 1728, whilst sailing from Kiliwhimen for Inverness, Wade (promoted to lieutenant-general the previous year) and the crew were caught in 'a most violent and terrible Hurricane … which continuing above 13 Hours the Vessel was … in the Most imminent Danger of being drove on the Rocks and dashed to pieces'. In the event, all made it safely to shore.

Wade had a dual reason for being in the Great Glen that summer. Inspecting progress on his new road from Fort William to Inverness was his chief object, but he was also taking the opportunity of advancing his plans for two new garrison forts – one at Inverness Castle and the other at Kiliwhimen. If anything possibly vied with the roads in Wade's affections it was these two mighty forts.

53 The Tay Bridge at Aberfeldy, designed by William Adam, built in 1733 and Wade's proudest achievement in his road-building programme.

54 *Garva Bridge, carrying the military road over the River Spey from Ruthven Barracks to Fort Augustus. The bridge and its associated road crossing the Corrieyairack Pass are very probably depicted in the background of van Diest's portrait of Field-Marshall Wade (see* **colour plate 7***).*

A fort for the king and a fort for the king's son

Fort George in Inverness, affectionately known by the Board of Ordnance as George's Fort, was founded on 7 August 1727. Wade named it in honour of his new king, George II, who had ascended the throne just two months earlier. Captain John Romer, engineer to the Board of Ordnance, was its architect.

The site chosen was the hill on which the medieval castle had stood (55). The place had been abandoned as a garrison and replaced by a citadel, 'Oliver's Fort', in Cromwell's time,

but this too had been forsaken following Charles II's return. With the accession of William and Mary in 1690, Mackay once again established a garrison and he opted to return to the ancient castle mound overlooking the River Ness from its eastern bank, most probably because it had a much greater command of the town. He made use of a lofty late-medieval tower house that still stood on the site and incorporated some neglected medieval defences into a new scheme of fortification. But by 1719 this fort too had passed its 'sell-by date'. The tower house, described as a 'mansion house' in a Board of Ordnance plan, was roofless and ruined, the defences were looking decidely threadbare and the well was choked with debris.

Wade had identified the need for a better garrison fort at Inverness right at the outset. That the Jacobites in the 1719 Rising had intended the Highland capital as their first major

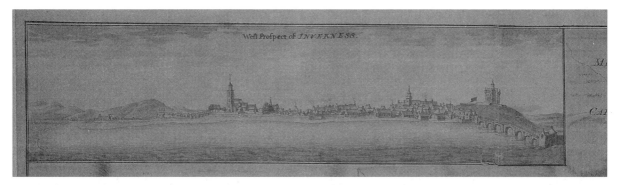

55 *A view of Inverness and the River Ness, from a Board of Ordnance drawing. The tower house of the medieval castle dominates the skyline.*

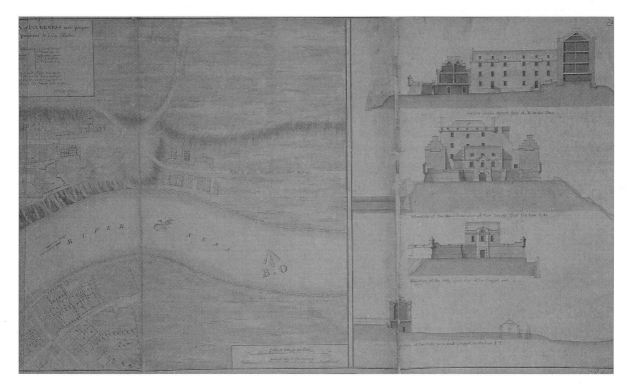

56 *John Romer's proposals for converting the medieval castle at Inverness into a new fort, to be called Fort George.*

objective after Eilean Donan doubtless confirmed him in this view. He invited Romer to prepare a scheme (**56**) for a garrison of six companies (about 400 men).

Romer chose to retain the lofty five-storey tower house, somewhat surprisingly in view of its vulnerability to artillery fire, though financial constraints might well have forced his hand. He even extended it on the west and the whole building became quarters for the officers and gunners. The rest of the fort was all Romer's creation, including a three-storey soldiers' barrack along the east side of the parade, a two-storey governor's house along the north side incorporating the main gate, and a powder magazine and chapel in a two-storey block along the south. These new buildings made attractive use of those Georgian

57 *Fort Augustus* (centre) *at the southern end of Loch Ness. The military road linking Fort Augustus with Fort George Inverness is in the foreground, just uphill from the present B862.*

architectural forms then in vogue – stepped gables, raised quoins and jambs – foreshadowing what Romer had in mind for the infinitely more impressive Fort Augustus (57).

Wade had hinted that he was unhappy with the small barracks at Kiliwhimen at the outset of his mission. It was 'situate at too great a distance from Lake Ness' for his liking, making it more difficult to keep supplied during siege. Fort William, at the south end of the Great Glen, and Fort George, at the north end, could both be provisioned directly from the sea but land-locked Kiliwhimen, 'reckoned to be the most centrical point of the habitable part of the Highlands' was vulnerable. Something had to be done.

Wade clearly toyed with the idea of substantially upgrading Kiliwhimen. A drawing in the Wade Collection shows James Smith's barracks given two new projecting towers at the corners lacking them and the whole complex doubled in size (58). But the idea was never followed through, and instead an entirely new fort was built down by the loch side. Wade named it Fort Augustus in honour of George II's third son, William Augustus. In 1726, at the tender age of five, this chubby lad had been created Duke of Cumberland; 20 years later the Highlanders would bestow on him a quite different title – The Butcher!

Fort Augustus was to be no ordinary garrison fort; it was to serve as the headquarters of the Hanoverian Army in the Highlands, and its governor was to have chief command over all the garrisons in the Highlands, including Fort William and Fort George, as well as the newly-raised Independent Companies (**59** and **colour plate 8**). Construction work began in August 1729 and such was the magnitude of the place that the fortress was not completed until 1742, by which date Wade, now a full general, had left Scotland never to return. Sadly, precious little of the fort survives today in any recognisable form, but the surviving Board of Ordnance plans and drawings dispel any doubt that the place was to be anything other than an awesome display of Hanoverian military might combined with an impressive architectural power. Romer was again chosen as architect, and Fort Augustus was undoubt-

edly his greatest contribution in his time as engineer to the Board of Ordnance in Scotland.

The fort was conceived on the grand scale. As a military work it consisted of four massive stone-faced bastions linked by four curtains. Each bastion (**60**) terminated towards the field in a sentinel box that became Romer's hallmark (see **62–3**). Beyond was an elaborate ensemble of outworks including a ditch, covered way and glacis. But somehow, despite this awesome display of military engineering, it is Fort Augustus's architecture that impresses more, in particular, the way in which the four building blocks, one on each side of the central parade, contrive to overwhelm the defence. Romer had each block projecting ever so slightly from the curtain, and made even more adroit use of Georgian details than he had

58 *A Board of Ordnance plan detailing proposals to upgrade Kiliwhimen Barracks. The scheme was abandoned by Wade in favour of a smart, new fort, to be named Fort Augustus.*

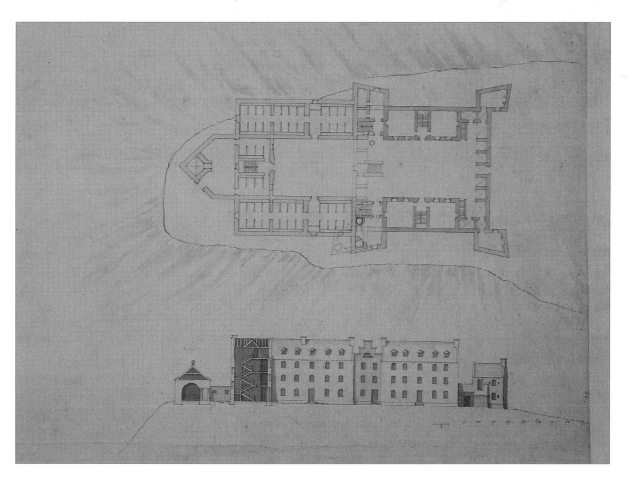

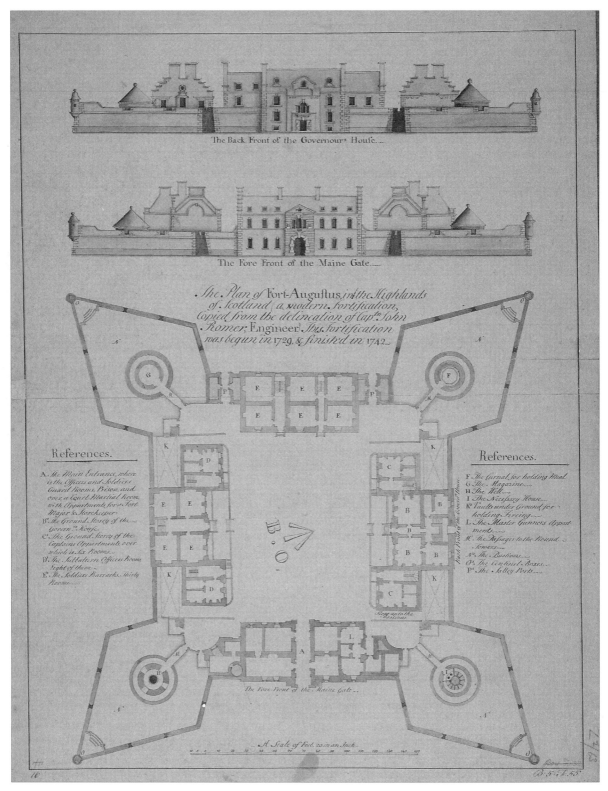

59 *John Romer's grandiose scheme for Fort Augustus.*

60 *The sole remaining bastion at Fort Augustus with the late-Victorian abbey buildings beyond.*

done previously at Fort George. These included Venetian windows over the two main entrances and oilettes for the dormers. Even the conical roofs of the four pavilions buried in the bastions and the ogee roofs of the sentinal boxes, all topped with stone balls, added to the grandeur. It seems strange then to discover that the barrack block at least was roofed with thatch 'which in rainy weather drips incessantly'.

Fort Augustus was designed to accommodate the governor, the permanent staff officers (fort-major, master gunner and storekeeper) and five companies (about 300 men), all within the four piles of buildings ranged around the parade. The only permanent buildings outside the fort were the governor's and officers' stables and a bakehouse and brewhouse, both placed beside the harbour

next to the River Tarff. The series of very detailed plans drawn up by Romer shows how they were disposed about the complex. Of particular interest are the four pavilions in the bastions and used as storage – well, girnel (grain store), necessary house (latrine) and powder magazine. It was this last that was to prove the fort's undoing.

New wine in old bottles

Wade and Romer did not put all their eggs in one basket and concentrate solely on Forts George and Augustus; they pursued a policy of improving all the chief garrison places as the circumstances and finances allowed. Elsewhere in the Highlands, for example, Fort William continued to be upgraded, though most of the much-needed work had been carried out prior to Wade's arrival. At Ruthven in 1734 Wade 'erected and built in a workmanlike and substantial manner a stable for 30 Dragoons with

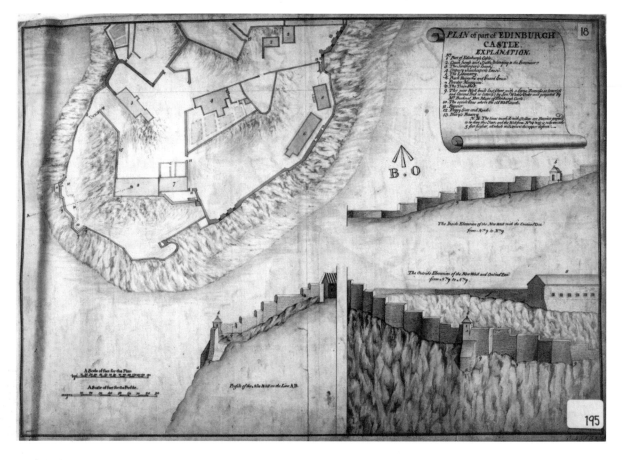

61 *A Board of Ordnance plan detailing early improvements to the Western Defences of Edinburgh Castle.*

all conveniences thereunto belonging, together with a guard-house for the security thereof'. This plain structure still survives roofless but otherwise complete, with an attic over the two-chambered stable. Recent excavation showed only 28 stalls, and evidence for a hitching rail along the front of the building either side of the stone forestair leading to the loft. At the rear were two outshot buildings, probably the tack-rooms.

Their energies, however, were concentrated most on the great royal castles in the Lowlands, once mighty seats of power but now perceived to be vulnerable to the Jacobite threat. That stark fact had been forcibly brought home to the Hanoverian Government

in the first days of the '15 Rising when crass incompetence alone thwarted the Jacobites' attempt to take Edinburgh Castle for the Pretender. A short note on one of the first plans drawn up by the Board of Ordnance after Wade's arrival highlights the concern: 'Orillon where ye Rebels attempted to surprise ye Castle in ye year 1715.' The postern gate beside the orillion (see **17**) had by this date already been 'closed up'. During their careers in Scotland Wade and Romer transformed the antiquated royal castles at Edinburgh and Dumbarton into acceptable 'modern' garrison fortresses, and much of what today's visitors see at both places is their work (**colour plate 9**).

The concerns were two-fold: defence and accommodation. There had been, of course,

62 *Typical sentinel boxes by John Romer on the northern defences at Edinburgh Castle.*

63 *King George's Battery and the Governor's House at Dumbarton Castle, both built in 1735 to designs by John Romer.*

considerable works – new defensive circuits and better accommodation – carried out to both castles in the latter half of the seventeenth century, which had adequately clothed the medieval fortresses in a more acceptable garb. But nothing is forever in this world and the continuing Jacobite threat, coupled with the changes in the Army establishment and structure, forced rethinks and imposed new requirements.

Take defence, for example. The Georgian military architect, seeing a wall with a curve in it, instantly wanted to straighten it out. A curve meant a 'blind spot' for the defenders. It was the presence of such a curved wall along the Western Defences at Edinburgh Castle that no doubt prompted the Jacobites to make their ascent from that side. Now that wall had only been built in the later seventeenth century as an orillion, or projection from the curtain, intended to cover the postern gate. Viscount Dundee and the Duke of Gordon must have had their secret conversation in its shadow in 1689. By Wade's time the orillion was perceived to be a weakness and not a strength and during the late 1720s and early '30s it was removed and the entire Western Defences 'ironed out' (61). The programme of works was carried round along the whole of the northern side also, and the complex, zigzagged artillery fortification there today is entirely a product of this campaign. A similar comprehensive programme of 'ironing out' was undertaken at Dumbarton Castle at the same time. At both places the intention was to provide a defence capable of resisting an assault supported by a limited artillery train, but not a full 'siege royal'.

The building work at Edinburgh Castle was carried out by William Adam, the noted architect but here working in his other occupation as master mason to the Board of Ordnance; in those days a man might be an architect as well as a building contractor. The Adams family business, working from its base in Leith, covered the whole of Scotland for the Crown.

Arguably its most notable achievement in this sphere was the Tay Bridge carrying Wade's road over that river just to the north of Aberfeldy (see 53). That bridge was designed as well as built by Adam, but this was exceptional. Usually, all designs and architectural details were a matter for the Board of Ordnance's engineer, and in Romer's case the most notable features were those attractive domed sentinel boxes which give Dumbarton and Edinburgh Castles that extra special flourish (62).

Wade, Romer and Adam also combined to upgrade the garrison accommodation. At Edinburgh, in 1737 the interior of the Great Hall, already serving as a soldiers' barracks, was substantially upgraded. Three storeys of accommodation were created within the towering height of James IV's majestic former banqueting hall and so hiding from view the impressive hammer-beam roof. Six large barrack rooms, two per floor, provided space for 310 men. At Dumbarton, in 1735 a splendid new Governor's House was built on the site of the demolished medieval gatehouse (63). The even more splendid Governor's House at Edinburgh, designed by Dugal Campbell, was built in 1742, by which date both Wade and Romer had left Scotland for pastures new.

Whilst Wade was deliberating in 1724 about what he might build at Scotland's great royal castles, there was another gentleman preoccupied in the same pursuit. The Earl of Mar, he who had lost the '15 Rising for the Jacobites, was by this time in exile. Perhaps he was at the court of the Pretender in Rome on 31 December 1720 when the news broke that his king, James VIII, had been presented with an heir, Charles Edward, 'Bonnie Prince Charlie'. Mar had clearly not given up the ambition of seeing the Stuart dynasty restored to the throne of Great Britain and Ireland. Having singularly failed to achieve that end through his military ability, or rather lack of it, he was now using his more considerable

Designe for Improveing the front of the Royall Palace in Stirling Castle, built by King James 5th. This front looks towards Edinbrugh Southeast. Paris Aprile 1724.

64 *One of the Earl of Mar's designs 'for improveing the front of the Royall Palace in Stirling Castle', drawn up in 1724 whilst in exile.*

skills as an architect to ensure that when that great day came James VIII should have a royal palace in Scotland fit for any king. As hereditary keeper of Stirling Castle he could be forgiven for choosing this royal fortress as the location. An extraordinary series of drawings for the Palace was drawn up by him, all showing great flair and imagination (**64**). But it was not to be. Neither Mar nor James was fated to return to the land of his birth, and it fell to Prince Charles, the Young Pretender, to attempt to achieve that end.

CHAPTER SIX

Culloden and the End of a Dream

It was surely wrong to sett up the Royal Standard without having the posetive assurance from His Most Christian Majesty that he would assist you with all his might.

(Lord George Murray writing to Prince Charles Edward Stuart from Ruthven Barracks the day after the Battle of Culloden)

The 1745 Rising

On 16 April 1746, on a windswept moor a little to the east of Inverness, Lord George Murray, the brilliant Jacobite general of the 1745 Rising, had to endure seeing his brave but half-starved soldiers fight a numerically larger and fitter army in an insane set-piece battle, on ground that he knew was 'not proper for Highlanders'. The Battle of Culloden was the last fought on British soil and proved to be the death-knell not only for thousands of Jacobites but also for Jacobitism itself. Murray's bitter words to his king summed up the feeling of betrayal the defeated Jacobites felt as they gathered at Ruthven Barracks (see **43** and **front cover**) after the battle, betrayal both by Prince Charles (**65**) for his deceit and by the French for failing to support the Rising.

The '45 Rising was entirely different from the far more threatening '15. Although perhaps the majority of Scots in their hearts and upbringing held some sympathy for the House of Stuart, it was increasingly the case that signs of the economic advantage of the Union

were beginning to seep through. The great landowners in particular had much to lose. Several notable supporters of the '15, like Lord Seaforth the Mackenzie chief, had

65 *Prince Charles Edward Stuart; by Louis-Gabriel Blanchet. The portrait hangs in the Royal Dining Room of the Palace of Holyroodhouse, where the Prince held court in the early days of the 1745 Rising.*

66 *William Augustus, Duke of Cumberland, sketched by Lieutenant-Colonel George Townshend, about 1750.*

successfully rehabilitated themselves and knew all too well that they would not get another such chance.

In 1739 Jacobite support received a much-needed boost with the outbreak of the War of Jenkins' Ear between Britain and Spain coupled with rumours of a possible war with France. The leading Jacobites were all agreed that for a Rising to succeed it must be supported by the French king, with at least 6000 regular soldiers, arms sufficient for 10,000 men and a substantial purse to boot. With none of this forthcoming, the '45 was never going to attract widespread support.

Ironically, it was the defeat of the British Army, led by the Duke of Cumberland (66), at Fontenoy in May 1745 that saved the Hanoverians from the indignity of a French invasion; why trounce the British in an away match when they could do it in front of a home crowd? But Prince Charles would not be deterred. He raised sufficient money to mount a small expedition but when he arrived at Eriskay in the Western Isles on 23 July, all but

alone, he was met with little enthusiasm. He was advised to return home by the two Skye chiefs, MacDonald of Sleat and MacLeod of MacLeod. 'I am come home', he retorted and managed to persuade MacDonald of Kinlochmoidart, Clanranald, MacDonell of Keppoch and Cameron of Lochiel to join him.

The Stuart standard was raised at Glenfinnan, in Clanranald's lands at the head of Loch Shiel, on 19 August. Just three days earlier the first shots of the '45 had been fired less than 20 miles away during a skirmish at General Wade's High Bridge over the River Spean on the road between Fort William and Fort Augustus; the Jacobites had won the first of their several encounters with the Redcoats. Recruiting continued in earnest, and when the army had reached 1500 men it moved eastward to gather more. In great haste Lieutenant-General Sir John Cope, General Wade's next-but-one successor, and his small force marched forth from Edinburgh Castle.

Cope's prime objective was to keep the 'wyld heighland men' out of the Lowlands, but his army was in a lamentable state. He had two inexperienced regiments and another that had seen at least some action. In addition, he had the dubious advantage of having nine companies of raw recruits raised initially for the Flanders killing fields and two regiments of Irish Dragoons with untrained horses. Although similar in size to Argyll's army in the '15, it was, if anything, worse prepared. But what of the Highland Companies, so recently raised and newly regimented? They were away serving in Flanders; even when they were returned to assist in the crisis the Government did not trust their loyalty and kept them in Kent until the damage was done. And what of the Highland forts and barracks so recently and so expensively completed? They were all so undermanned that their garrisons could do nothing other than sit and watch as the Prince's army marched past, ironically availing itself of the military roads so kindly provided by the Hanoverians! The Jacobite army, with

67 The Palace of Holyroodhouse, where Prince Charles Edward Stuart held court in the early days of the 1745 Rising and where the Duke of Cumberland resided after the Battle of Culloden before returning to London.

north, and instead of heading westward over the Corrieyairack Pass to meet up with the Fort Augustus garrison and face the rebels he continued on to Inverness where his troops immediately embarked for Edinburgh. The Jacobite army moved on unchecked and, on its triumphant way to the capital city, Bonnie Prince Charlie was lavishly entertained at the ancient Stewart Palace of Linlithgow; the palace fountain ran with red wine. The city of Edinburgh, though not its castle, fell very quickly, and while most of the Government officials made their hasty exit southward to the safety of Berwick's great walls, Prince Charles Edward established his court temporarily at the Palace of Holyroodhouse (**67**). The place buzzed with excitement (**68**), with a grand ball, assemblies and entertainments. Bonnie Prince Charlie's youthful charm won many a heart in those heady early days of the Rising, but it was winning the war that mattered most. A promising start was made on 21 September, when Cope's army, fresh from its sea voyage, was soundly beaten in ten minutes flat at the Battle of Prestonpans, a little to the east of Edinburgh. Scotland was recovered for the Stuarts, and more recruits to the cause poured in from the north.

insufficient guns to attempt to take the larger forts, was content to leave these meagre garrisons in its rear. Even the smaller barracks proved stubborn. Only Inversnaid was successfully taken. At Ruthven, the 12 brave men stationed there under Sergeant Molloy's leadership withstood the might of 300 Jacobites for two days (see **44**), losing only one man who, according to 'the dashing red sergeant' in his account to Cope of the attack, had been 'shot through the head, by foolishly holding his head too high over the parapet'! Of such hardened souls was the British Army made.

Cope headed for Ruthven in Badenoch, hoping to supplement his forces from the strongly Whig areas of the north and east. It failed to materialise, and so too did the expected battle. Cope lost his nerve on the road

But divisions were already developing. Charles was jealous of the leadership qualities of Lord George Murray and tried to replace him. The Highland officers would have none of it, and to a man they refused to fight for anyone else. But Murray was outvoted on the question of whether to invade England, and the Jacobite army marched south. Such a move suited the French perfectly; a distraction at England's postern gate. For the move into England to be successful, the Scottish Jacobites were dependent on support coming from English Jacobites, but their doors stayed tight shut. When the army reached Swarkestone Bridge over the River Trent near Derby, sense prevailed and they wheeled round and marched north again. The London Government was in a state of panic, further compounded by intelligence reports coming in of an impending French invasion of the south coast of England. The Duke of Cumberland's army in the south was put on alert and General Wade's army, then at Newcastle, ordered to attack. But Wade was on the wrong side of the Pennines and bitter weather prevented him from reaching the returning Jacobites. Unbeaten and unbowed, Prince Charles's army returned to Scotland in good order and won a further victory at Falkirk on 17 January 1746 before entering the Highlands once more. The Duke of Cumberland's army followed on its trail, some of his troops bivouacking in Linlithgow Palace where Bonnie Prince Charlie had so recently held court. As the redcoats quit their quarters on 1 February they carelessly left their great fires burning and the palace went up in flames.

By now the Jacobite army was short of money and supplies and after an abortive and foolish attempt by the ludicrous Mirabelle de

Gordon on Stirling Castle they were forced back to the Highlands. Their goal was Inverness. In the by-going they attacked Ruthven Barracks again and this time Gordon of Glenbucket ('de gread Glenbogged' as George II was wont to call his feared Jacobite opponent) and his 300 men took it. The army then set to work on Fort George. Major Grant, the garrison commander, shamefully surrendered his 200 men after barely two days of persistent undermining by his namesake Colonel Grant, an Irish Jacobite engineer. The Jacobite army now split into two, with Cameron of Lochiel and MacDonald of Keppoch leading a force to blockade Fort William, that blight on the Cameron landscape for almost a century, and Brigadier Stapleton setting out to besiege Fort Augustus. The garrison at Fort William resisted but the mighty Fort Augustus fell almost immediately when one lucky mortar bomb blew apart the powder magazine in the northwest bastion. The garrison commander, Major Wentworth, followed Major Grant's lead and surrendered, though an attempt to send the disgraced garrison as prisoners of war to

68 The Jacobite army encamped in Holyrood Park.

69 *A Board of Ordnance plan of Fort William under siege in 1746. The Jacobite gun batteries are shown emplaced on the high ground to the east* (left) *of the fort.*

France failed when they escaped from their prison in Nairn. Meanwhile Stapleton and Grant moved down the Great Glen to assist with the attack on Fort William, but with Colonel Scott in command it proved a much tougher nut to crack. He trained his guns on the Jacobite batteries emplaced on higher ground to the east of the fort, injuring Grant and leaving the inept Mirabelle de Gordon once again in control of the guns (**69**). The siege was lifted as the extent of the retaliation against the Cameron kinsmen became known and the need to join the Prince for his planned battle became urgent. That retaliation, chiefly in the shape of attacks on isolated communities, was blamed on Argyll's men; but the

Camerons were just the first to get a taste of what the Hanoverian forces were to mete out to many.

Charles was now firmly of the opinion that only a great victory in battle would return a Stuart to the throne, and thus he forced his tired troops into the guns of Cumberland's 8800 men at Culloden (**colour plate 10**). When it dawned on him that failure was obvious, he was led from the field. The remnants of the Jacobite army with their leaders regrouped at Ruthven Barracks and over the next few days waited for word from their would-be king. On the 20th his message arrived: 'Let every man seek his own safety in the best way he can.' Chevalier Johnstone expressed the emotions that beat in the hearts of all those present that day: 'This answer, under existing circumstances, was as inconsiderate in Charles as it was heart-breaking to the brave men, who had sacrificed themselves in his cause.' It was the

70 *The Duke of Cumberland's army encamped at Fort Augustus in 1746; by Paul Sandby. On the left side of the fort is the ruined bastion where the powder magazine was located before taking a direct hit from one of the Jacobite guns emplaced on the high ground to the left.*

end of a lost cause.

'Butcher Cumberland' made doubly sure it was the end, and the backlash was as brutal as it was indiscriminate. Cumberland began earning his soubriquet of 'Butcher' on the bloody field of Culloden, where the Jacobite wounded were mercilessly slaughtered. He then led his army, now reinforced with four more regiments, as they thundered round the Highlands and down the Great Glen like a tornado (**70**). By September 1746, there were 15,000 Government troops in Scotland, most of them in the Highlands and ordered into the glens to burn and pillage at random. There could be no mistaking the Government's determination to ensure such a rebellion would never happen again.

A Disarming Act was hurriedly passed, which banned not only Highland weapons but also the wearing of tartan and the kilt and the playing of the bagpipes. It was rigorously enforced. The penny had finally dropped that Westminster must take Scottish opposition seriously, and to control it required money and men. When Cumberland resigned as Commander-in-Chief in March 1747, to be replaced by the Earl of Albermarle, the army numbers remained the same. That did not change until General Bland succeeded Albermarle later that year. Even then he had nine regiments of foot, thirteen Highland Companies and two regiments of dragoons at his disposal – a policing force similar to Cromwell's. This created logistical problems of accommodation, with only the old royal castles and Fort William capable of providing barrack space. As a result, every town and village had troops quartered on them. But something more permanent had to be done, and fast (**71**).

A second Fort George

The spectacle of two of King George's three Great Glen forts in ruins was a humiliating reminder of the ineffectiveness of past systems of defence. That they had fallen so easily was even more humbling. They must be quickly rebuilt. Fort Augustus was rebuilt and given an elaborate new defence, though whether these outworks were ever finished must remain in doubt. Fort William likewise was repaired and a temporary timber barracks built outside it to house 160 men. But poor Fort George in Inverness (**72**) was 'intirely in ruins', thanks to

a French artillery sergeant named L'Epine who had laid mines under selected parts after the garrison surrendered and blown the place to bits, himself included! What was to be done with this once-proud symbol of Hanoverian supremacy?

The first thought was to replace it by abandoning Castle Hill and rebuilding Cromwell's citadel down by the harbour. A plan was drawn up by Major Lewis Marcell, an Irish engineer, in 1746, followed the year after

71 *The military places of strength and roads 1745–69 (Chris Unwin).*

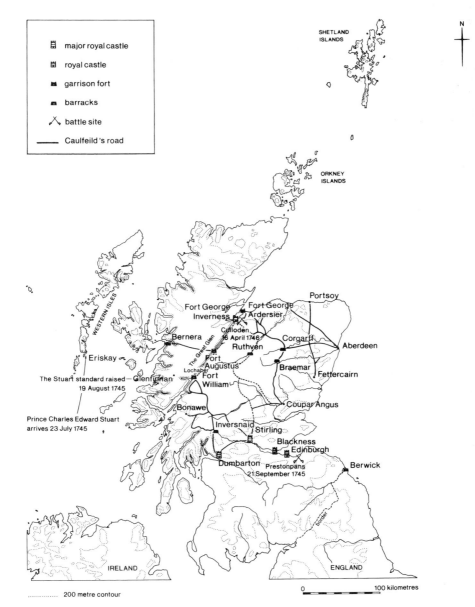

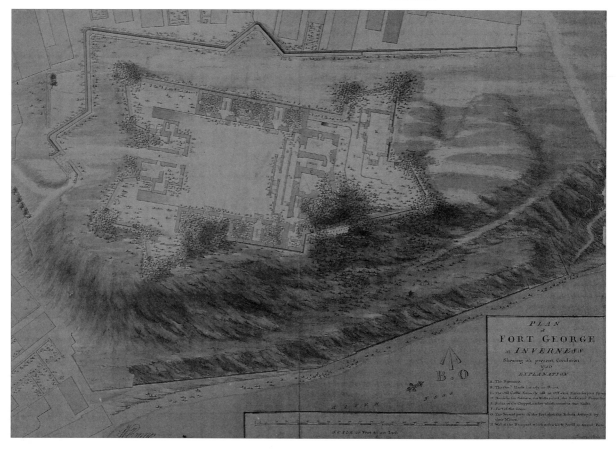

72 *A Board of Ordnance drawing of Fort George Inverness, showing the devastation caused by the Jacobites shortly before Culloden.*

by another scheme, this time drawn up by the newly-appointed engineer for the Board of Ordnance in North Britain, Major-General William Skinner. The building contract was agreed with William Adam. However, at the last minute Inverness Burgh Council claimed compensation of several thousands of pounds because of loss of use of their harbour, with the result that Skinner was instructed to look for another site. Late in 1747 he drew up his plan for what Lieutenant-Colonel James Wolfe, veteran of Culloden and soon to be hero of Quebec, described as 'the most considerable fortress and best situated in Great Britain'.

Skinner chose the windswept point of Ardersier, a shingle spit of land jutting into the Moray Firth from the southern shore 10 miles to the east of Inverness and just five miles from Culloden. This unpromising site, barren save for a little hut, was on loyal Lord Cawdor's land and surrounded by estates owned by lairds who had remained faithful to the House of Hanover throughout, including Forbes of Culloden himself. The virgin site gave Skinner free rein to explore every avenue and what he conceived for the new Fort George was an artillery fortification and army garrison on a monumental scale, at once impressive and terrifying to an enemy. It is a credit to Skinner that his design changed very little between that first drawing in 1747 and the completion of the fort 20 years later, by which date George II had passed the way of all flesh and a third George sat on the throne. Only one new building was added in all of that time, the garrison chapel. Indeed, since the eighteenth century there has been only one major addition, the 1930s' NAAFI (**73** and **colour plate 11**).

Fort George Ardersier was designed to accommodate two infantry battalions (about 1600 officers and men), a detachment of artillery, staff officers and fort officials, including the governor. The estimated cost was £92,673 19s 1d. William Adam again won the contract but he died in 1748 before work got underway and it fell to his three sons, John, Robert and James, to continue the work. Indeed, some of the details betray more than a hint of Adam influence; Robert, the most famous son, at least was cutting his teeth at

the Fort, and by all accounts hating every minute of it!

Building the fort was not easy. The place covered 42 acres (17ha), all of the materials had to be brought in by sea and it would take more than 1000 men to build. It was the biggest single building project ever undertaken in the Highlands and remained so until the Caledonian Canal was constructed in the following century. The stone came across the Moray Firth from quarries in the Black Isle, the timber from Whig estates at Avoch, Fowlis and Balnagowan, much of the ironwork from Edinburgh whilst merchants in Inverness supplied most of the nails, lead and tools. Bricks were made on site.

Labour was a problem. Most of the skilled workforce had to be brought from the Lowlands, even from Ireland, but in those pre-JCB days the huge amounts of earth-moving had to

73 *A plan by William Skinner of Fort George Ardersier, dated 1749, charting the progress of the building work.*

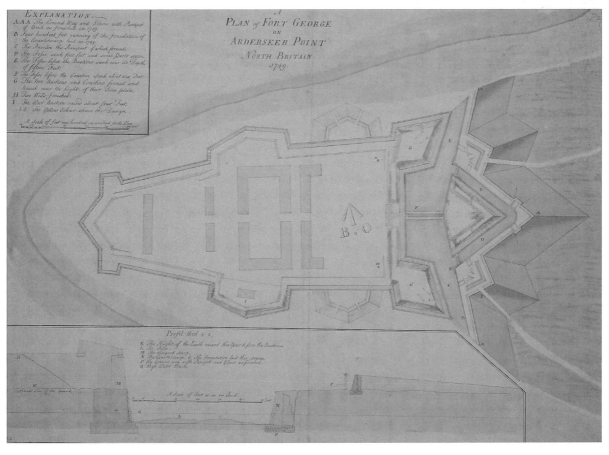

74 *The eastern defences at Fort George, viewed from the Prince of Wales's Bastion. On the left is the principal bridge and on the right the ravelin bridge; in the centre the ravelin itself with its guardhouse.*

be done by hand, and the creation of the great bastioned defences which overawe visitors today took thousands of men and thousands of wheelbarrows. This unskilled workforce was provided by the army, in much the same way that the military roads were constructed. In 1749, Barrel's Regiment was detailed 'to carry on the fortifications at Ardersier Point ... [it] must encamp and must have at least two days free from all work.' This was no enlightened employer offering days of rest, but one ensuring that the men were free 'in order to exercise' so that they were still equipped for their main task, fighting.

Because of the importance to the new fort of the sea, the harbour was one of the first things to be built after the workmen's huts. Then building began in earnest on the eastern defences, to close off the narrow spit of land on its one landward side (**74**). The headland was protected by a temporary palisade while the permanent triangular-shaped ravelin that would protect the main entry was completed. The ravelin also had the short-term advantage of forming a safe redoubt while the remainder of the fort was being built. In 1753, it was armed with eight guns whilst eight more were perched on top of the great mounds of earth being thrown up out of the ditch to form the east wall of the fort. The fortifications demonstrate the superb technical skill William Skinner had learned during his military career, first from his adopted father, Captain Talbot

Edwards, in Barbados and the Leeward Islands, and later from some of the best engineers in Gibraltar, Minorca and Devonport. The simple epithet on his gravestone perhaps sums up his career best:

> To the Memory of Lieutenant-General William Skinner, who died 1780 having served sixty-one years an engineer, twenty-three of which as chief engineer of Great Britain.

The form of angled-bastioned defence he used had changed little in the 40 years since he began his career. Similar work could be seen at Fort Augustus and at Tilbury in Essex, but the scale of Fort George was excitingly new. Skinner was honoured for his achievement by being appointed the fort's first governor.

As the work progressed, the urgency to complete the fort ebbed, but it received a gentle jolt in 1759 with the threat of a French invasion. Needless to say this raised the spectre of yet another Jacobite Rising, and as a precaution the Government ordered an additional regiment to the fort along with artillerymen and guns. The complete armament was put in place in the following year. Attuning himself to the heightened possibility of an attack from the sea, Skinner altered the seaward Point Battery into a casemated gun battery to cover the narrow sea channel between Ardersier and Chanonry Point in the Black Isle.

As work on the fortifications progressed, the garrison buildings began to rise from their shingle bed. The two enormous piles of barracks were begun first, in 1753. Together they took 11 years to construct and, like Berwick Barracks before them, were occupied before they could be properly finished. After the barracks came the grand magazine, quickly built between 1757 and 1759 to hold 2500 barrels of powder; Skinner ensured that it had a thick, brick-vaulted roof sufficient to withstand a direct hit from a mortar bomb, clearly learning the lesson of the wrecked magazine at Fort Augustus. The twin ordnance stores followed (1759–61) (75), then the two provision stores

75 *The twin ordnance stores at Fort George.*

(1760–2), housing also lodgings for the garrison baker and brewer. The two splendid staff blocks that today form such a magnificent backdrop to the parade's grassy sward as one enters the fort were built between 1762 and 1766 (**colour plate 12**). Finally, and only when every other building was under way, did work begin on the chapel (**76**). Skinner almost certainly intended to build a chapel from the outset; he was, after all, effectively creating a small town of 2000 people, about a quarter of the size of Inverness at the time. The fort would not have been complete without one, the more so as Sunday service was compulsory under Army regulations.

76 *The interior of the garrison chapel at Fort George.*

The Latin inscription over the chancel arch in the chapel reads: 'George III, by the grace of God King of Great Britain, France and Ireland, 1767'. The work to complete this second Fort George had taken far longer than expected and cost far more than intended (**77**). In fact, the final bill came in at over £200,000 (over £1 billion, at today's prices), more than twice the original estimate. We can only assume that the House of Hanover thought the price worth paying; it was after all more than the annual Gross National Product for Scotland at that time.

Garrison life

Fort George was to provide for all the needs of its large garrison and Skinner's time as barrack

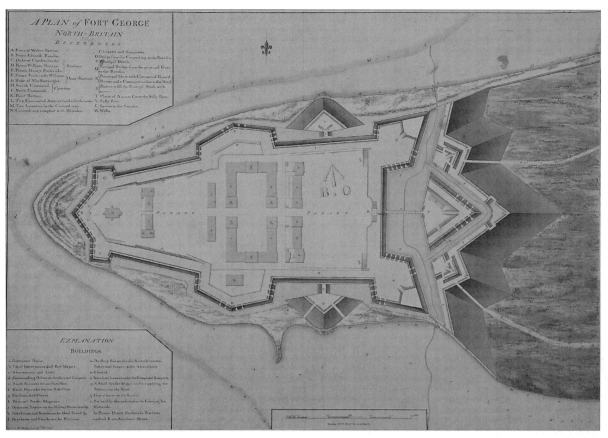

77 William Skinner's final plan of Fort George, dated 1769, showing the completed fortress.

master in Gibraltar must have helped him considerably in this task. The officers' lodgings in the barrack blocks were more spacious and more refined, as befitting their occupants' superior rank. The subtle architectural details emphasise the difference. Externally, their quarters were in pavilions set forward from the ranges occupied by the rank and file, the central blocks housing the senior officers further enhanced with decorated pediments. Even the windows lighting the officers' accommodation had larger panes of glass. Within, the rooms were pleasingly, if somewhat spartanly, furnished with nice fireplaces, panelled doors and window shutters; the stairs were given nicely turned balusters.

The barrack rooms for the rank and file by contrast were poky (**78**). Each contained four double beds, a table and two forms. There was a good-sized fireplace but this was used for cooking as well as for heating. The men still had no communal messing, washing or recreational facilities provided and they perforce spent much of their time in their rooms. This might appear somewhat rough from our cosy modern perspective but in truth this was what the soldier might expect in a contemporary inn and much more than he got either under canvas or in stables, which was where many a soldier was quartered. Improvements came by and by; a garrison inn was created out of former officers' lodgings, as well as a school, sutler's shop, post room and hospital.

The rank and file were not allowed to marry except with their commanding officer's consent, and then only one in a hundred men was permitted to 'marry on the strength', where his wife would receive half rations in return for washing duties. But judging by the

78 *A soldiers' barrack room at Fort George, reconstructed as it might have looked in 1780. The men slept two to a bed, eight to a room, cooking, eating, sleeping and relaxing there. One in a hundred soldiers was allowed to 'marry on the strength' and have his wife and any family staying with him in the same room!*

frequent reiteration of the rule forbidding women from the barrack room this was obviously ignored. No married quarters were provided by the Army, but if spare rooms were available they might be used but only at the discretion of the commanding officer. Otherwise, a corner of the barrack room was screened off with a blanket.

The Hanoverian Army in the Highlands

Fort George was conceived as a great garrison fortress shielding the might of the Hanoverian Army. But it was no more than a bolt-hole for the troops and more positive measures were required to strike terror into the heart of every Highlander. Cumberland, therefore, instigated a policy of frequent army patrols sallying forth from regularly garrisoned barracks, a ploy that Cromwell had used with success. To this end, surveys were carried out by the Board of Ordnance of many castles and forts to assess whether they might be put to good use. The Board was fortunate in being able to call on the services of the brothers Thomas and Paul Sandby, renowned artists in their own right. Thomas had recently painted the Battle of Culloden for the Board (see **colour plate 10**), though he somehow managed to make it look for all the world like a shinty match; now they both set out on their travels and produced wonderful views of Fort Augustus and some of the more remote island castles like Duart and Tioram for the survey (**colour plate 13**).

Armed with these surveys, Colonel Watson for the Board proposed several schemes for controlling the inaccessible areas of the Highlands. He listed an impressive number of potential outposts strung out along the glens and lochs and over the hill passes which would he maintained put a stranglehold on all movement in the Highlands. He was in a good position to understand the problem of communication in the Highlands through his work with Major Caulfeild, Wade's successor as the surveyor of military roads. It was Watson and his assistant, a young Lanarkshire lad, William Roy, who produced the first topographical maps of Scotland. His *Report for Cantoning the Five Highland Companies in the Western Highlands and Remoter Parts of the Islands*, written in 1747, was typical of his well-planned schemes. It meticulously plotted the necessary outposts, the number of soldiers required at each, and the proposed means of supply. He further recommended removing the regular troops from Bernera Barracks (see **colour plate 6**) and replacing them with Highlanders who could be outposted across that region. He also made the point that 'the service proposed must entirely depend on the Spirit, Vigilance and Activity of the Officers'.

The patrols were to be relieved every fortnight, and each man was to be issued with 24 rounds of ammunition and sufficient supplies.

The outposts were to be located from Aberdeenshire in the east to the Western Isles. Castles like Braemar, Duart and Mingary were pressed into use and additional summer stations were set up at places like the head of Loch Arkaig, on Loch Laggan, at Tomintoul, in the Braes of Angus, Loch Morar, Loch Rannoch, Loch Leagh and Loch Lag. Until well into the 1750s, the Highlands were saturated by them. Each outpost was manned by a company commanded by a junior officer, either a captain or an ensign. A number of patrols, each about five or six strong and led by a non-commissioned officer, skirted around the boundary of the outpost, all keeping

within a few hours walk of each other.

A typical outpost was that established at Corgarff Castle in western Aberdeenshire (**79** and **colour plate 14**). This simple sixteenth-century tower house was 'to be occupied by the regular troops in the Highlands to put the laws in execution for disarming the Highlanders suppressing their dress and for preventing Depredations'. The castle had seen action during the Jacobite troubles: in 1690 the Master of Forbes wrote that the castle of Braemar was burnt, 'as also the castle of Curgarff, which is burnt of late. If orders be given [to repair them] I shall sei it done.' Corgarff served as a rendezvous point for Jacobites during the '15 and 30 years later, at the outset of the '45, it again served for a staging post as the Jacobite army marched past Braemar into Atholl. Weapons were brought from Strathbogie and stashed in Corgarff to supply the march, but before they could be

79 *Corgarff Castle surrounded by its star-shaped wall.*

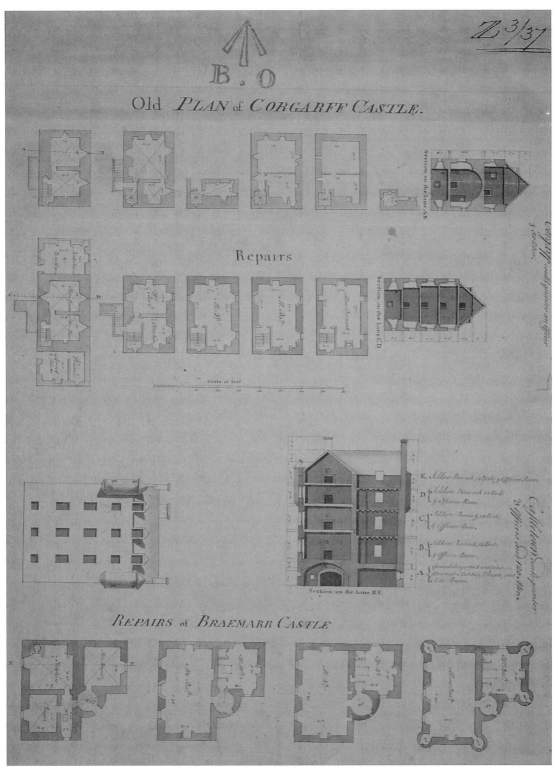

80 *Plans of Corgarff and Braemar castles showing proposals for their conversion into acceptable army barracks.*

used the castle was raided by a party of Government troops under Lord Ancram's command. One of Ancram's officers recalled how the 300 foot and 100 dragoons had marched:

> … over the mountains and Moors almost impassable at any time of the year, but much more so when covered with snow [to a castle] which stands on the side of the Don, where I daresay never Dragoons were before, nor ever will be again, nor foot either, unless Highlanders! Though we marched early in the morning it was past four before we arrived there. We found it abandoned by the Garrison, but so lately, that the fire was burning, and no living creature in the house but a poor cat sitting by the fire.

The account goes on to tell how they destroyed 32 double barrels of excellent powder and burned 200 muskets, taking 131 away with them to Aberdeen. Their return journey left its mark on the narrator: 'We were obliged to be two nights in the open fields – and sit upon horseback all night.' All right for the dragoons, but what about the poor foot soldiers?

Corgarff was now altered to take a company of infantry (**80**). Skinner, scaling down his thoughts from the dizzy height of creating mighty Fort George, designed the alterations and John Adam was contracted to undertake the work, which began in 1748. The inside of the small tower house was completely gutted. The stone-vaulted hall ceiling was taken down and an extra floor inserted, making five storeys in all. The old newel stair was similarly removed and replaced by a timber scale-and-platt stair. Small pavilions were added to either side of the tower to provide a guardroom and prison in one and a bakehouse and brewhouse in the other. This little outpost was protected by a star-shaped wall loopholed for musketry. So far as we know, it was never put to the test.

While the building work on site progressed, orders were placed by Thomas Leslie, barrack master for North Britain, for beds, other furniture and bedding. Alexander Peter was contracted to copy the pattern furniture held in Edinburgh Castle, and Thomas Gairdner and William Taylor were to make the bedding, comprising canvas beds [mattresses] stuffed with flocks, bolsters, sheets, blankets and coverlets. Interestingly, replacement beds were also to go to Bernera, Inversnaid and Fort Augustus in the same contract. By 1750, Ensign Rutherford and a detachment of 45 men from Pulteney's 13th Foot were in residence; those blankets and coverlets would be sorely needed when the winter snows came.

About half the garrison based at Corgarff was permanently away from the barracks at any one time. These patrols either billeted on the locals or stayed in barns. Although the patrols were within reach of each other, supplying them was a serious problem. Food was scarce throughout the Highlands and all too often 'they [could] get little or nothing but meal in the country'. Similar worries were expressed by many officers stationed throughout the Highlands. Captain Hugh, reporting from the head of Loch Rannoch in August 1749, wrote that, 'since my last, I have left a command of six men at Lock Arkeg and moved to this station for the convenience of provision and meal, which could come no longer at Arkeg on account of the waters, having left what meal I had with the party there, with management may serve them four weeks.' Another problem was drink, but this was not due to its short supply. On the contrary, there was too much of it, it was quite cheap and the soldiers had a lot of time to drink it!

The task these outposted garrisons were instructed to carry out verged at times on the inane. The various captains' reports paint a ludicrous picture of red-coated soldiers chasing Highlanders over the hills to arrest them for wearing a kilt or carrying a targe – and frequently losing their catch. If the aim was to destabilise and dehumanise the population it probably failed; for the most part the High-landers ran rings round the patrols. But they were undoubtedly an intrusion and a nuisance in the glens, and a great many extra mouths to feed.

A typical patrol area with its headquarters at Laggan Achadrom was commanded by Captain Molesworth. In his report for June 1750 he listed his patrols as follows:

Laggan Achadrom	miles	cap	sub	ser	corp	men
HQ		1		1	1	10
Head of Glen Morrison	9		1		1	8
Knochlin Height of Strathglass	8			1		6
Strath Cluney	8			1		8
Head of Glenshiel	9				1	6
Balachan between Lochs Garry and Quick	12				1	6
Garvimore and Garvibeg	18			1		6
Leach Roy, head of Glen Roy	7				1	5
Head of Glen Spean	10				1	5
High Bridge	10				1	5
Nine mile Bridge	3				1	4
moving patrol	3		1	1	1	

He records that he advertised his orders on the church doors in his district, and that 'the country seems quiet and all the parties detached from me have remained without any information of Cattle stolen, nor have they found any person in highland dress.' For his past cases he tells us that he 'took up Arbd. Kennedy with a Cow and Calf in his possession, and sent him prisoner to Inverness, where he was committed to jail by the sheriff but since Bailed. The Cow and Calf remain in my Custody... The 1st June my party recovered a Horse Stolen from Alexdr. McDonell of

Strathglass and restored him to his owner, they persued the thief who was armed and in Highland Dress, but Night coming on he escaped in a wood.'

Some of these patrols went on despite doubts raised as early as 1751 of their efficiency. While Mull was abandoned, additional barracks were built at Rannoch, because 'the party of the King's Troops which are stationed at the head of Loch Rannoch during the summer and harvest are very badly accommodate both as to Quarters and Provisions; there is now [1751] a Commodius House to be built immediately for the Officers; Two rooms in front and a Parlour, with one wing for a Kitchen and the other for a stable; as also a barrack for the soldiers near by the House.' A note in the margin estimated the cost between £15 and £20. As usual it was an underestimation, since the 'barrack alone cost near £100'. It was paid for by the Commissioners for Forfeited Estates. Other houses may also have been altered or built, including no doubt the King's House at Garvamore, at the eastern foot of the Corrieyairack Pass, one of the better billets.

One interesting snippet of evidence of life in these outposts has recently come to light in the form of a plan attached to the claim by Norman MacLeod of MacLeod for compensation for the barrack land at Bernera (81). This plan shows the position of the barracks, the land where the soldiers cut their peats, their garden ground and a series of over a dozen small huts on the road from the barracks to Glenelg that are described as the huts for the soldiers' wives and families. As we saw at Fort George, few women were allowed to live in barracks and the army did not provide married quarters, so these huts may have been built by the soldiers themselves. This plan, drawn in 1748, is one of the earliest illustrations of quarters for army families. As the huts represent a time of stability in the garrison they probably pre-date the '45 Rising.

The pacification of the Jacobite clans in the

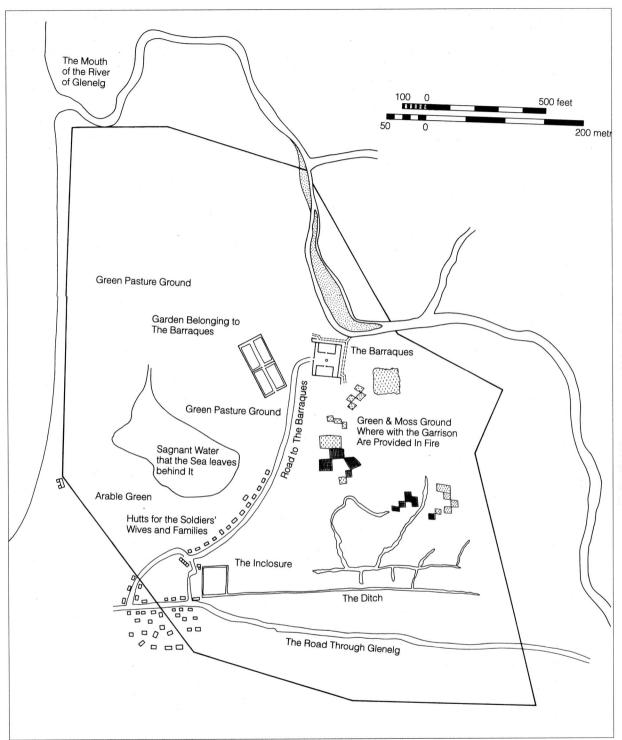

81 *A sketch plan* (redrawn from the original by Chris Unwin) *showing the barracks at Bernera and the ground about them. The plan shows huts for the soldiers' wives and families beside the track leading from the barracks to the village of Glenelg, a very rare and early acknowledgement of the need for such accommodation.*

82 *Dumbarton Castle from the River Clyde.*

Highlands was achieved not solely by the Highland garrisons; the Lowland bases at the castles of Edinburgh, Stirling, Dumbarton and Blackness, and Berwick Barracks, played their part as well. In the aftermath of Culloden, all were 'stuffed with men'. The majority were stationed there over the long winter months; during the spring they packed their knapsacks and headed for the glens, either to work on the roads, patrol the glens or relieve the Highland garrisons. At Edinburgh the numbers were so great that a special building had to be hastily erected in 1746 beside Mills Mount Battery to hold the provision carts bringing up supplies to the troops from the town. This little building, which helped fill the bellies of the Redcoats, now sustains today's visitors in a similar way as the Mills Mount cafe and restaurant! Elsewhere in the castle almost every available space was pressed into service to accommodate the troops. Even the tiny closet in the former royal palace where the Stuart king, James VI and I, had been born in June 1566 was unceremoniously turned into a small-arms store in the Hanoverian cause. Only the locked Crown Room in the palace, where the Scottish Crown Jewels, the Honours of Scotland, had been secreted away after the Union in 1707, escaped Army occupation. New buildings perforce had to be erected. A new barracks was built along the north side of Palace Yard in 1755 and the rank and file doubtless thanked the Lord as they emerged

83 *The 1748 powder magazine crouching inside its blast wall on the Beak at Dumbarton Castle.*

from the darkened vaults beneath the Great Hall that had been their home since the 1730s. (That barracks now serves as the Scottish National War Memorial.) A new powder magazine and two ordnance stores appeared behind Dugal Campbell's Governor's House. It was a similar story at the other royal garrisons, and particularly good powder magazines surviving at Dumbarton (**82, 83**) and Berwick are living testimony to this.

Gradually, as the Jacobite threat evaporated, these large garrisons, in Highlands and Lowlands alike, were reduced. The pressing need now was for soldiers on foreign soil and the home garrisons increasingly became manned by the Invalid Companies (**colour plate 15**). These were a little like an eighteenth-century 'Dad's Army', soldiers too old or infirm to continue serving in their regiments. They had first been formed into independent companies in 1708 during Marlborough's campaigns when the Army required every possible able-bodied man to serve abroad but realised that home garrisons were crucial. The Invalids became the regular garrison troops across Britain, and by the 1750s they were present in all the Scottish forts and barracks (**84**).

A muster return of the Invalids in the Scottish royal castles for 1752 poignantly illustrates the composition of these companies. Those in Edinburgh Castle, for example, were aged between 46 and 79 and suffered variously from 'blindness and deafness', 'swelled legs', 'incurable and hurt in the breast', 'wounded at Culloden and not recovered', 'lame and one arm', 'diseased with vermin and a sore leg', 'deliriously sickly and a bad leg', 'very deaf sickly and old' and lastly, but certainly by no means least, two with 'gravel and ruptured'. It beggars belief how they might have coped had the French invaded!

By 1757, the cost of supplying these garrisons, particularly those in the Highlands and the Western Isles, was causing Mr Leslie, the barrack master for Scotland, some concern.

84 *The gravestone in the Craigs Burial Ground at Fort William of Neil McFarlane, 'late invalid in Fort William who died 3 June 1801 aged 55 years'.*

And as the Jacobite threat receded, so the necessity of having this elaborate organisation was called into question. Lord Beauclerk wrote:

> It has been usual for these several years past to send parties on what is called the Highland Duty, who occupied several stations from the beginning of June till the later end of Nov. to suppress Depredations and inforce the laws against the Highland Dress and Arms.
>
> Considering the great number of idle men who have by recruiting been lately drain'd out of the Highlands, the detaching these Parties may probably be thought unnecessary; and I should myself be of this opinion were it not for the uncommon Dearth and Security which at present prevails in the Highlands, whereby Reports, the People are said to be nearly in a starving condition.

The garrison outposts did continue, but the ones that survived after the outbreak of the Seven Years' War were those which assisted the fight against smuggling.

The only winners from the vast sums of money expended in the Highlands in the middle years of the eighteenth century were the road users. Major Caulfield, Wade's successor as road builder, spent £130,000 and employed many thousands of soldiers between

1740 and 1767 building 900 or so miles of road (**85, 86**). He truly opened up the Highlands, realising perhaps Wade's real dream for his roads, not as aiding troop movements but as assisting the economy of the Highlands, for by that route was he convinced peace would come.

As 'Butcher Cumberland' set about his work after Culloden, Bonnie Prince Charlie slipped out of Scotland a sad and lonely figure. He was destined never to inspire another Rising, just legends and a lot of romantic songs. The Highlanders were cowed but resilient, and they soon discovered that the Hanoverian Government offered them new opportunities to exercise their considerable skills as fighting men – in the service of the burgeoning British Empire.

85 *An inscription at the Well of the Lecht, beside the military road to the north of Corgarff Castle, recording that five companies of the 33rd Regiment under their colonel, Lord Charles Hay, made the stretch of road between there and the River Spey in 1754. That road is still in use as the A939.*

86 *Invercauld Bridge, the finest surviving bridge on the military road built 1749–54 between Blairgowrie and Fort George.*

CHAPTER SEVEN

The Enemy Without

I sought for merit wherever it was to be found; it is my boast that I was the first minister who looked for it and found it in the mountains of the north. I called it forth, and drew into your service a hardy and intrepid race of men, who became a prey to the artifice of your enemies, and had gone nigh to have overturned the State. These men ... were brought to combat on your side; they served with fidelity, as they fought with valour, and conquered for you in every part of the world.

(William Pitt, Earl of Chatham, writing to George III in 1766)

Jacobites and the army of Empire

Pitt's modest boast had the bare bones of truth in it. During his ministry many Scottish regiments were raised and sent abroad with indecent haste on a conveyor-belt system to feed Britain's new-found imperial success. Regiments were needed for Europe, Africa, India and the Americas. England had always been a difficult recruiting ground, and recruiting sergeants frequently had to resort to devious means to ensure a man would wake up in the morning with the 'king's shilling' in his pocket. Once hooked there was no escape. The volunteers Sergeant Kite hoped to get when he beat his drum in 1704 were the disadvantaged: 'if any 'prentices have severe master, any children have undutiful parents; if any servant too little wages or any husband

too much wife' then they could always find an escape in the Army. But all too often it was necessary to bribe men to enlist, and even then, during times of war, they had to resort to pressing men into service. This did not improve the standard of recruit, nor did giving convicted criminals the option to serve king and country as an alternative to punishment. The problems of recruiting in England increased proportionately with the expansion of the Empire. More recruits had to be found, not only to form new regiments but also to reinforce existing units depleted by long years of service overseas. The notion of recruiting from the large populations in the straths and glens had its obvious pitfalls but it also had its clear attractions.

The first to consider pressing Jacobites to fight overseas was an American colonial, Sir William Pepperrell. In 1745 he was given a commission to raise a regiment amongst the colonials living at Louisberg. It proved such a difficult task that the regiment had still not reached its full complement in 1748. In his frustration, in 1746 he wrote to the Duke of Newcastle suggesting that some of the 'Rebell prisoners, who may have been unwarily seduced' into the '45 Rising might be of great help to him in making up his numbers.

Scotland was an obvious place to turn to for recruits. The butchery over with, there were a great many brave young men ready for the taking. The old social and economic order in the Highlands had begun to decline even before the '45, and the Disarming Act and Tenures Abolition Act of 1746 accelerated this pattern. The menfolk were now unable to dress in their normal clothes or to carry their usual weapons, but more importantly the ties binding them to their clan chief were loosening. There was also a large reservoir to draw from. A demographic study commissioned by the Government from the Reverend Webster, minister of the Tron Kirk in Edinburgh and a staunch Whig, indicated that 51% of the Scottish population resided in the area north of the Tay, with well over 30% in the Gaelic-speaking areas. Webster's study separated out the men of fighting age, between 18 and 58, from younger boys deemed too immature to fight and those older men who had a tendency to be 'Crazy and Infirm'. By his reckoning the able-bodied formed a fifth of the population, giving a figure of 12,000 effective men in the Jacobite heartlands. Although Lord President Dundas gave no reason for wanting this survey (there was no such study carried out elsewhere in Britain), there can be no doubt that it prompted not a few recruiting regiments into looking greedily northwards. These facts, combined with the Scottish landed class emerging from yet another Rising with yet more debt, and a pressing need both to raise money and, just as importantly, a desire to regain their status, all led to a rise in the popularity of the Army as a career.

The principle of raising Highland troops to fight overseas was not entirely new. Highland officers were by then an accepted part of the British Army. Between 1707 and 1750 a quarter of all officers appointed to the British Army were Scottish. Some, like the second Duke of Argyll, the first Earl of Orkney and the second Earl of Stair, had sparkling careers, reaching the very highest ranks. During the 1740s, both the Duke of Argyll and the Earl of Loudon raised companies to serve in the War of Austrian Succession. There was also the success of the Black Watch. Originating as the

four Independent Companies, or Watches, established at Wade's request in the 1720s, they had combined in 1739 to form the Earl of Crawford's Regiment of Foot. The new regiment was kitted out in a Government tartan woven in black, dark green and blue, which was to give it its present name (see **colour plate 15**). Although initially raised for home service, it was persuaded abroad and fought in Cumberland's Army at Fontenoy in 1745. The real breakthrough, however, came in 1756 when the British Government, faced with a further war in Europe and mounting trouble in the Americas, simply had to find a new recruiting ground. The Black Watch were posted to America, but before they went they had a very significant change of colonel when their Campbell commander was promoted to the 54th Regiment and Major Francis Grant was appointed in his place. Grant was a younger brother of Ludovick Grant of Grant who had displayed the most lukewarm allegiance to the House of Hanover during the '45. The young major was now determined to do what so many were to emulate, regain his family's reputation in the eyes of the Government through military service. Shortly afterwards, a second Highland corps was raised by Archibald Montgomerie, an Ayrshire Whig who had married a sister of the Skye chief, MacDonald of Sleat. With his brother-in-law's influence in the Highlands he had no difficulty raising almost 1500 men. They shipped out to Halifax in Nova Scotia without even the rudiments of basic training.

There was no question where Montgomerie's loyalties lay, but the urgent need for yet more and more fighting men required the Government to take a gamble on the questionable loyalties of others. An instance was the commission issued to Simon Fraser, the son of the scheming 'Spider of Dounie', Lord Lovat, who had been captured at Culloden and executed. The Master of Lovat had also been caught and imprisoned in Edinburgh Castle for his part in the Rising, but the

Government accepted that he had been embroiled reluctantly into the Jacobite cause. His willingness to embrace the Hanoverian cause enabled him to secure his release from Edinburgh Castle on the promise of his living in Glasgow, far removed from his family's forfeited Inverness-shire estates. He did so with gusto, throwing himself into training for a legal career, and his new-found loyalty was repaid when he was given command of one of the first two regiments to be raised for the war in America. Fraser's Highlanders, or the old 78th Regiment of Foot, were raised largely from the forfeited estates of his family, with the rest coming from neighbouring estates. Fraser used the new regiment not only to establish himself but also to help his fellow Highland peers. The list of officers serving with the 78th reveals the names of numerous men who needed to prove that their coats had turned for good and all. Among them were John Macpherson, the brother of Cluny Macpherson, Donald MacDonald, the brother of Clanranald, and John MacDonell of Lochgarry, who reconciled himself sufficiently well to be given the command of MacDonald's 76th Foot when it was raised in 1777. Fraser of Lovat himself went on to even greater heights, reaching the rank of major-general and succeeding politically where his father had failed, sitting as the Member of Parliament for Inverness until his death in 1782. He also contrived to have his family's forfeited estates granted back to him by a special Act of Parliament, acknowledgement that his military achievements had earned him 'some particular act of grace'.

The recruitment of erstwhile Jacobites into the British Army was a bitter pill for the Hanoverian Government to have to swallow and, to help the medicine down, it insisted that the ever-loyal Campbell Duke of Argyll must 'vet' those officers raising companies who would then 'be sent to America as soon as they are raised; and none will be suffered to remain in the Country on any pretence'. Despite this,

the success of the recruiting sergeant was remarkable. And yet, when the Seven Years' War ended in 1763, most regiments were disbanded, much to the irritation of Pitt, who saw the reduction of the army from 120,00 to 30,000 as brutal when it would leave some of the 'bravest men the world ever saw' to 'starve in country villages'. He also recognised the waste of trained manpower that this represented, considering that they would 'forget their prowess'. Several of these regiments were disbanded in America and many of the soldiers chose to stay there and set up home, some eventually to fight against Britain during the War of Independence that followed.

Defending the realm

The diminishing of Jacobite disaffection in the Highlands during the 1750s and '60s enabled the major garrisons to be substantially scaled down in size and the number of outposts to be reduced. The Invalids, despite their obvious deficiencies, were still deemed capable of poking a musket through a loop should the need arise. Fortunately for them, not to say for the nation's security, the possibility was remote. The powerful armament emplaced at mighty Fort George was never called on to fire a shot in anger.

The Invalids were clearly not expected to take over all the home duties of the regular army – road building, assisting at the repair and rebuilding of the forts and barracks, patrolling the glens. By the time Fort George was finished in 1767, that rebuilding programme was over and the road network complete. Only the need for the patrols continued, though on a much reduced basis. The last Jacobite to pay with his head, Alan Cameron, the brother of Lochiel, was captured in 1753 by the Inversnaid garrison. But as the Jacobite threat receded a new problem appeared in the glens to ensure that patrols continued to be needed until well into the following century – the illicit distilling and smuggling of whisky.

The defence of Scotland generally, whether from whisky smugglers or French soldiers, was a vexed issue. The reduction in the number of regular troops stationed there now left Scotland vulnerable. One option was to do as the English did and raise militia regiments locally, but King George was emphatically opposed to arming the populace of Scotland. The question of raising militia regiments in Scotland became an important intellectual debating topic, involved as it was with the people's right to defend themselves and Scotland's right to be trusted as a loyal nation. But it was not until 1797 that the Scottish Militia Act was passed and even then it may not have been so much a means of allowing the Scots to defend themselves as a ruse by the Government to raise and train a pool of soldiers to send to fight Napoleon.

From 1759 fencible regiments had been raised to act as a home defence but they were not raised through local initiatives but on behalf of the Government, much as the line regiments (**87**). Their conditions of service may have dictated that they were only obliged to serve within Britain, and they were initially issued with pikes because of a shortage of muskets, but soldiers serving in fencible regiments were put under great pressure by a voracious Westminster Government to transfer to the line regiments due to embark for overseas service. The Government's need to raise and replenish foreign service regiments led to basic lies being told about their conditions of service, lies which, when tumbled to by the rank and file, led down the road to mutiny. Between 1743 and 1800, 16 Scottish regiments felt no recourse other than to mutiny, chiefly after being threatened with service overseas. Despite this reputation for mutiny, the Highland regiments became respected as among the best fighting men in the British Army. Discipline was seldom a problem, at least as long as the number of Highland officers remained in proportion to the soldiers. They were brave, in the view of

87 *Sir James Grant, chief of Clan Grant and Lord-Lieutenant of Inverness-shire, takes the salute of the Strathspey Fencible Regiment which he had raised in 1793; by John Kay.*

General Wolfe to the point of foolhardiness, and like most soldiers recruited from the rural areas they were more inclined to be self-sufficient and resourceful.

Perhaps the most intriguing aspect of the raising of the Highland regiments is that they were allowed to wear the kilt, the banning of which had been so rigorously enforced after Culloden. Why they were granted such a privilege is not clear. No other part of the British Isles was permitted to make fast and loose with so fundamental a part of Army discipline as the uniform, by now regulated to the last button and bow. The Duke of Cumberland had specifically commissioned drawings of each regiment's uniforms, which were published in the *Clothing Book*. The only rational explanation seems to be that it was a very effective recruiting incentive. And incentives were certainly needed if an incident from the raising of the Atholl Volunteers is to be believed. A gentleman 'in a journey through Athole' one morning observed a poor fellow running to the hills as for his life, closely pursued by half a dozen of human blood hounds. Turning to his guide the gentleman anxiously inquired the meaning of what he saw. 'Och,' replied the imperturbable Celt, 'it's only the Duke raising the Athole "volunteers".'

Despite these little local difficulties, recruiting was undoubtedly a success. In the last quarter of the eighteenth century, 20 Highland regiments were embodied into the British Army, over half of which have survived to form the core of the famous Scots regiments of today. From a Jacobite viewpoint, the most significant acknowledgement of their accept-

ance was the raising of the Cameron Highlanders in 1793. By now Fort George, Fort William and the royal castles had shed their garrison role by and large and become important recruiting bases for the new regiments (**88**). The monumental – and it has to be said, monumentally gross – New Barracks built in Edinburgh Castle in the 1790s to house an infantry battalion is tangible proof of this burgeoning British Army.

The only entirely new fort to be built other than Fort George was Fort Charlotte in the 1780s (**89**). We first encountered a fortification beside the Bressay Sound in Shetland in the mid seventeenth century, built to defend this important northern harbour against a European threat. With the arrival of American privateers, led by the renegade Lowland Scot,

88 *The 79th Highlanders march out through Foog's Gate, Edinburgh Castle, in 1853; by R.R. McIan.*

89 *Fort Charlotte from the air.*

John Paul Jones, and founder of the American Navy, off the coast in 1779, the Government was persuaded that it was in its interest to re-establish a garrison there.

The new Fort Charlotte was built on the same site and almost on the same lines as the earlier fort. It was garrisoned by 270 men of the Sutherland Fencibles. Within the fort was a barrack pile with eight rooms for 26 men each with a corresponding number of officers' rooms in the pavilions. A north pile contained the officers' kitchen and mess and the com-manding officer's lodging. A magazine and ammunition stores were built as well as artificers' rooms. But once again it proved a questionable investment. By 1797 the garrison was being reduced, and by the time of Walter Scott's visit in 1814 the two companies of Invalids then in occupation were about to be withdrawn. The writing was on the wall for the Highland garrisons.

The end of the line

In 1807 Cardinal Henry Stuart, the late Bonnie Prince Charlie's younger brother, and the last Stuart claimant to the throne of Great Britain and Ireland, passed peacefully away in his Italian residence. During his dotage, Henry had been comforted by a generous pension from the Hanoverian king. That single gesture effectively buried Jacobitism for good.

The nineteenth century proved the end for the Highland garrisons also, with the excep-tion of Fort George. It was to be a long, ling-ering death. In 1817, in the euphoria that followed Waterloo, an order to dismantle all the Highland forts was given and then countermanded. In 1835 the Board commis-sioned a report on them all in an attempt to relieve itself of their upkeep. Fort George was suggested as a suitable place for a civil prison. Already it had been pressed into use as a gaol for political prisoners from Ireland, and the place had even been advanced as a suitable

90 *Fort William from the south shortly before much of it was swept away in 1889 to make room for the new railway terminus. The main gate, seen here still in its original position, was taken down and re-erected in 1896 at the Craigs Burial Ground, the former soldiers' cemetery, a short distance from the fort.*

place to incarcerate Napoleon; in the event he was exiled to an island in the Mid Atlantic, but to the London Government there was probably little to choose between the two, both were equally remote. The prison idea never came to anything and the fort continued as a recruiting base and basic training camp.

Forts William and Augustus were not so lucky. In 1864, Mackay's masterpiece was sold to Mrs Cameron Campbell, whose very name shows how the world had changed, and the final ignominy came in 1889 when it was purchased by the West Highland Railway Company (**90**). Much of the fort was unceremoniously swept away, cheered on no doubt by the locals still with the memory of the Glencoe massacre in their hearts, to make room for engine sheds; just one block of officers' barracks was retained for housing railway workers. In 1867, Fort Augustus was sold back to the Frasers of Lovat (how would the 'Spider of Dounie' have relished that

91 *A piper of the Queen's Own Highlanders in the barrack square at Fort George, 1988.*

115

moment?), and they now used it partly to house tenants and partly as a shooting lodge until the fifteenth Lord Lovat gave it to the Benedictines in 1876 for use as a monastery, which it remains today. The monastic layout is remarkably similar to Romer's original plan and some at least of his barracks may survive beneath the hallowed plaster. By then all the minor garrisons throughout the Highlands and Islands had long been abandoned. The last to pass out of the Board's care was tiny Corgarff in 1831, its shelf-life extended because of a pressing need to control the illicit distilling and smuggling of whisky in Strathdon. By the end of the century, only mighty Fort George and the Lowland royal castles continued under Army occupation (**91**).

92 *'What a difference 250 years make!';* *'Glenfinnan charge!' – a modern cartoon of the '45 Jacobite Rising* (Maurice Scott Cameron).

Let the last words be left to that closet Jacobite, Dr Samuel Johnson, who with his friend and biographer, James Boswell, visited Fort George in 1773 and feasted handsomely at the governor's table:

> It is true, that I cannot now curse the house of Hanover; nor would it be decent for me to drink King James's health in the wine that King George gives me money to pay for. But, Sir, I think that the pleasure of cursing the House of Hanover, and drinking King James's health, are amply overbalanced by three hundred pounds a year.

In one way or another it was what all the Jacobites had successfully done; eventually he who pays the piper calls the tune. The rehabilitation of the Scottish aristocracy into the administration of the British Empire in so short a time shows stunning adaptability and an astonishing skill at survival, at the cost of the blood of the 'wyld heighland men' (**92**).

"Perhaps drinking King George's health in that Glenfinnan pub was a mistake!"

Places to Visit

HS – Historic Scotland
NTS – National Trust for Scotland
EH – English Heritage

Battle sites

Killiecrankie (NTS) This sylvan setting was the site in 1689 of the first set-piece battle between the Jacobites and Government troops. The visitor centre, perched on a shelf of the glen, has models and maps of the battle, which ended in victory for the Jacobites but, tragically, also the death of their leader, 'Bonnie Dundee' (see **16**).

Glencoe (NTS) Not strictly speaking a battle site, but included here for completeness, this haunting glen – the 'Glen of Weeping' – was the place of the infamous massacre of 1692 when 38 men, women and children of the MacIans or MacDonalds of Glencoe were killed by soldiers from the garrison at Fort William (see **colour plate 3**). The visitor centre has a video programme on the massacre.

Glenshiel (NTS) The short-lived 1719 Rising ended at this battle site, dramatically situated in the shadow of the Five Sisters of Kintail, not far from Shiel Bridge at the head of Loch Duich (see **48**). An information board explains the story of this extraordinary Spanish-aided Rising. On the north shore of Loch Duich itself is Eilean Donan Castle (see **47**), the headquarters of the combined Jacobite-Spanish force before the battle. Bombardment by Government forces badly damaged the ancient castle and much of what the visitor sees today is restoration of the early twentieth century.

Prestonpans The site of Bonnie Prince Charlie's victory over Sir John 'Johnny' Cope in 1745 is now dominated by a grassy pyramid immediately to the east of Preston. Close by is the recently restored Bankton House, home of Colonel James Gardiner, one of Cope's officers.

Culloden (NTS) The site of the last battle fought on British soil, in which the Stuart dynasty's hopes of ever regaining the throne were finally dashed, has recently been restored to its state on that fateful day in April 1746 (see **colour plate 10**). The visitor centre has a colourful historical display and an excellent audio-visual programme telling the story of the '45 Rising.

Medieval castles

Edinburgh Castle (HS) Substantial remains from the period 1650–1750 survive, buildings as well as fortifications. The Dry Ditch at the top (west) end of the Esplanade originated in Cromwell's time, the perimeter wall skirting the western edge of the Upper Ward, loop-holed for artillery and musketry and containing the mysteriously-named Foog's Gate (see **88**), and the parapet of the Half-Moon Battery and the Forewall Battery from Charles II's time. Almost all the zigzag defences around the north, west and south edges of the castle rock date to the early eighteenth century (see **colour plate 9**), whilst many of the existing buildings owe their origin to this time, including the Queen Anne Building (1708), the Governor's House (1742), the Mills Mount Cartshed (1746) and the Ordnance Storehouses (1753). The North Barracks, built in Crown Square in 1755, forms the shell of the Scottish National War Memorial, opened in 1927. The gargantuan New Barracks (1796–9) that dominates the castle's skyline from the western side is clear evidence of the rapidly growing British Army during the Napoleonic Wars.

Stirling Castle (HS) The spectacular medieval buildings that make a visit to this royal castle so rewarding lurk behind impressive defences which date in the main to the time of the early Jacobite troubles of 1689 and 1708 (see **10**). Most imposing are the Outer Defences, built by Captain Dury between 1708 and 1714, which confront visitors as they approach from the Esplanade. James IV's great Forework and the nearby Elphinstone Tower owe their present stunted appearances to the fact that both were reduced in height and converted into gun platforms in the late seventeenth and early eighteenth centuries.

Dumbarton Castle (HS) Much of what the visitor sees today dates from the period 1650–1750 (see **82**). These include most of the surviving fortifications – the Spur Battery from Slezer's time, King George's Battery with its attractive sentinel box (see **63**) from 1735. The Governor's House was also built in 1735 and the Magazine on the Beak (see **83**) in 1748. The French Prison and most of the north-facing fortifications date from the later eighteenth century.

Blackness Castle (HS) Although only a minor garrison post, Blackness was kept in good repair and work of the period 1650–1750 is evident in the present remains. These include the superstructure of the Spur flanking the entrance (see **13**) with its massive iron yett, or gate, part of the repairs carried out in 1693. In the same year the North (Stern) Tower was reduced in height to its present stunted appearance to create a level platform for three heavy guns covering the seaward side. The accommodation within the Central (Mast) and South (Stem) Towers was altered for barrack accommodation in the following century.

Inverness Castle The site of the medieval castle, and of its eighteenth-century successor, the first Fort George (see **55** and **56**), is now occupied by the Sheriff Court and District Court, built in Queen Victoria's day. All that survives from a former time is the medieval castle well, restored in 1909.

Kilchurn Castle (HS) The ancestral seat of the Campbells of Glenorchy, this castle, magnificently situated at the northern end of Loch Awe in Argyll (see **colour plate 1**), was substantially remodelled for Sir John Campbell, first Earl of Breadalbane (see **24**), between 1690 and 1698, apparently to house his private army. The substantially complete ruin includes probably the earliest surviving purpose-built barrack block in mainland Britain.

Cromwellian citadels

Very little now remains of the five citadels built during the Cromwellian occupation – not surprisingly since they were intentionally dismantled after 1660. The best remains are at Ayr (National Grid Reference: NS334221) where substantial stretches of walling survive, particularly along the seaward flank. Only the gateway into Leith Citadel (NT267766) survives – just – tucked away in a corner near the junction of Dock Street with Commercial Street, whilst a clock tower (subsequently re-roofed) vies for attention with oil storage tanks in Inverness's harbour area (NJ664463). A rather scrappy remnant of citadel wall lurks nearby. Inverlochy Citadel was subsequently subsumed into Mackay's Fort William and nothing at all remains of the citadel in Perth, or for that matter the Jacobite entrenchments built there in the '15 Rising (see **colour plate 4**).

Government forts, barracks and roads

Fort William The fragmentary remains of this fort survive, largely lost and forgotten beyond the railway station, on the north side of the town which took its name from this once-formidable fortress. Begun in 1690, on the site of Cromwell's citadel at Inverlochy, and finally abandoned in 1864, only sections of the north and west rampart survive, including the sally-port and one demi-bastion (see **22**). The near-by Craigs Burial Ground has some interesting headstones recording members of the garrison (see **84**), and the main gateway into the fort, probably built in 1745 (certainly not in 1690 as the inscription gives) and relocated here in 1896. The West Highland Museum, in Cameron Square, has interesting information on the fort, including mid-eighteenth-century panelling removed when the Governor's House in the fort was demolished.

Ruthven Barracks (HS) This roofless but otherwise complete infantry barracks was built on the site of a medieval castle after the '15 Rising (see **43** and **front cover**). The stables were added in 1734. Captured by the Jacobite army early in 1746, Ruthven was where the remnant of that force gathered shortly after the defeat at Culloden.

Bernera Barracks The barracks built in 1719–23 beside the then main crossing from Skye to the mainland survives largely intact in this enchanting spot close by the village of Glenelg (see **46** and **colour plate 6**). The present road from Shiel Bridge to Glenelg mostly follows the line of the old military road. The car/passenger ferry (summer only) from Glenelg to Skye preserves this historic droving route.

Berwick Barracks (EH) The barracks built beside the Cow Port in the north-east quarter of the ancient walled town between 1717 and 1721 stands complete, together with the Clock Block of 1739–41 (see **38**). Berwick became the depot of the King's Own Borderers (now the King's Own Scottish Borderers) in 1881, and the barracks is still the regiment's headquarters and museum. The well-preserved powder magazine of 1749 stands nearby.

Fort Augustus The present Benedictine abbey, built over the great Hanoverian fortress completed in 1742, still preserves a few remnants from the fort's august past. Visible from the outside are the battered remains of the north-east bastion (see **60**), now minus its sentinel box, and the low footings of the north-west bastion, whilst on the inside may be seen the brick-vaulted guardrooms of the west range. Behind the nearby Lovat Arms Hotel in the town of Fort Augustus stands a stretch of musket-looped wall (see **45**), the sole surviving legacy from the earlier Kiliwhimen Barracks, built after the '15 Rising.

Fort George (HS) One of the outstanding fortifications in the British Isles, this monumentally impressive fortress was planned after the Battle of Culloden in 1746 as an impregnable base for George II's army, and completed in 1769 (see **colour plates 11** and **12**). The fort continues to serve as an army barracks but with its full complement of original garrison buildings and encircling artillery defences still intact. Inside the fort are reconstructed barrack rooms (see **78**) and guard rooms, the impressive Seafield Collection of arms and military accoutrements from the late eighteenth century, and the fine regimental museum of the Queen's Own Highlanders.

Fort Charlotte (HS) The rampart of the 1780s fort follows the outline of the fort begun but left incomplete in 1665–7 (see **89**). The 1780s garrison buildings remain substantially complete but modified over time.

Corgarff Castle (HS) This sixteenth-century tower house was greatly remodelled after the '45 Rising to house a company of soldiers outposted from Fort George (see **colour plate 14**). It has recently been restored, and attractive displays, including a reconstructed soldiers' barrack room and a whisky still, tell the story of this remote garrison. A little to the south of the castle a good stretch of the military road, built between 1749 and 1754 between Blairgowrie and Fort George, may be walked. Also worth a look in the by-going is the inscription (see **85**) at the Well of the Lecht, beside the A939 north of Corgarff, erected in 1754 by soldiers of the 33rd Regiment who worked on the military road to Fort George. Further down Strathdon from Corgarff are two medieval castles with Jacobite associations: Kildrummy Castle (HS), where the Earl of Mar made his final preparations for the 1715 Rising, and Glenbuchat Castle (HS), the residence of Gordon of Glenbucket, a stalwart Jacobite.

There are countless miles of military road to be walked, the most popular being those stretches included in the West Highland Way linking Glasgow with Fort William. The reader is referred to the excellent details in William Taylor's *The Military Roads in Scotland* (1976). Of especial interest are the following:

The Tay Bridge This was undoubtedly the finest of all Wade's bridges (see **53**). It was designed by William Adam, built in 1733 and is still used to carry the A846 over the River Tay just to the north of Aberfeldy

Invercauld Bridge (HS) This is the most impressive of the Caulfeild bridges to survive along the route of the Blairgowrie–Fort George military road built between 1749 and 1754 (see **86**). The bridge, built in 1753 and by-passed a century later, carried the road over the River Dee a little to the north of Braemar. Braemar Castle, like Corgarff a medieval tower house greatly remodelled after the '45 Rising, is also well worth a visit.

Glossary of Military Terms

The technical words given by military engineers to the various parts of a fortification, and mentioned in this book, are defined below.

bastion The strongpoint of an artillery fortification corresponding to a projecting tower of a medieval castle or town wall. All bastions have two faces meeting at an angle, and two flanks which join the faces to the curtains (see below).

caponier A covered passage across a defensive ditch through which musketeers could fire on the attacking force.

casemate Originally a stone-vaulted gun emplacement, but later extended to include accommodation protected from heavy artillery.

counterscarp The sloping wall forming the outer limit of a ditch.

covered way (or *chemin couvert*) The strip of ground making a defensive line beyond the ditch, not covered over but covered in the sense of being protected by fire from a parapet wall.

curtain The length of rampart between two bastions corresponding to the lofty stone wall between two towers of a medieval castle or town wall.

demi-bastion A half-bastion with one flank and one face.

embrasure An opening in a wall for cannon.

enfilade To fire at right angles to the parapet of a defensive position, so depriving the defenders of the protection of the parapet.

face The straight sides of a bastion or other work towards the field.

flank The walls of a bastion that join the faces to the curtain.

glacis A broad smoothly graded strip of ground falling in a gentle slope from the parapet wall of the covered way.

magazine A storehouse for military stores, usually gunpowder.

orillion A semicircular projection at the shoulder of a bastion intended to cover the guns and defenders on the flank.

palisade A fence of stakes, usually sharpened to a point so as to form a further obstacle.

parapet A breastwork, usually with sufficient earthwork in front of it to make it proof against cannon fire.

rampart The continuous work raised to surround a fortified place, and including bastions, demi-bastions and curtains.

ravelin A detached triangular work surrounded by its own ditch built in front of a curtain, generally at the entrance.

redoubt A field-work enclosed on all sides, its ditch not flanked from the parapet; an inner last retreat.

sallyport A gateway for troops to make a sally, or sudden rushing forth to attack besiegers.

scarp The sloping outer walls of the rampart and ravelin.

terreplein The broad level fighting platform on the rampart behind the parapet.

Further Reading

General history

William Ferguson, *1689 to the Present*, Edinburgh, 1975.

Gordon Donaldson, *James V–James VII*, Edinburgh, 1976.

Rosalind Mitchison, *Lordship to Patronage: Scotland 1603–1745*, London, 1983.

Michael Lynch, *Scotland: A New History*, London, 1991.

Cromwellian episode

C.H. Firth, *Scotland and the Protectorate*, Edinburgh, 1899.

F. Dow, *Cromwellian Scotland*, Edinburgh, 1979.

Jacobite risings

Paul Hopkins, *Glencoe and the End of the Highland War*, Edinburgh, 1986.

Sir Charles Petrie, *The Jacobite Movement*, London, 1959.

Bruce Lenman, *Jacobite Clans of the Great Glen 1650–1784*, London, 1984.

Bruce Lenman and John Gibson, *The Jacobite Threat – Rebellion and Conspiracy 1688–1759*, Edinburgh, 1990.

J.B. Salmond, *Wade in Scotland*, Edinburgh, 1938.

John Baynes, *The Jacobite Rising of 1715*, London, 1970.

Alistair and Henrietta Taylor, *1715: The Story of the Rising*, London, 1936.

The Sunday Mail *Story of Scotland*, Glasgow, 1984.

Military architecture

Andrew Saunders, *Fortress Britain: Artillery Fortification in the British Isles and Ireland*, London, 1989.

Stewart Cruden, *The Scottish Castle*, Edinburgh, 1981.

John Gifford, *The Buildings of Scotland: Highlands and Islands*, London, 1992.

G.P. Stell, 'Highland Garrisons 1717–23: Bernera Barracks', *Post-Medieval Archaeology*, 1973.

William Taylor, *The Military Roads in Scotland*, London, 1976.

G.R. Curtis, 'Roads and Bridges in the Scottish Highlands: the Route between Dunkeld and Inverness 1725–1925', *Proceedings of the Society of Antiquaries of Scotland*, 110, 1978-80.

R.A. Skelton, 'The Military Survey in Scotland 1747–55', *Scottish Geographical Magazine*, 83, 1962.

Iain MacIvor, *The Fortifications of Berwick-Upon-Tweed*, London, 1972.

Iain MacIvor, *Edinburgh Castle*, London, 1993.

Iain MacIvor, *Fort George*, Edinburgh, 1988.

I. MacPhaill, *Dumbarton Castle*, Edinburgh, 1979.

W.D. Simpson, 'Corgarff Castle', *Proceedings of the Society of Antiquaries of Scotland*, 61, 1926–7.

N. Fojut & D. Pringle, *The Ancient Monuments of Shetland*, Edinburgh, 1993.

Descriptions of certain sites are also to be found in the county *Inventories* of the Royal Commission on the Ancient and Historical Monuments of Scotland.

The Army

Peter Young, *The English Civil War Armies*, London, 1973.

John Child, *The Army of Charles II*, Manchester, 1976.

Michael Barthorp & G.A.Embleton, *The Jacobite Rebellions 1689–1745*, London, 1987.

John Child, *The Army, James II and the Glorious Revolution*, Manchester, 1980.

Norman MacDougall (ed), *Scotland at War 79–1918*, Edinburgh, 1991.

R.E. Scouller, *The Armies of Queen Anne*, Oxford, 1966.

Alan Guy, *Economy and Discipline: Officership and Administration in the British Army 1714–63*, Manchester, 1985.

J.A. Houlding, *Fit for Service: The Training of the British Army 1715–1795*, London, 1981.

Roy Palmer, *The Rambling Soldier*, London, 1977.

John Prebble, *Mutiny: Highland Regiments in Revolt 1743–1804*, London, 1977.

Finally, the authors recommend perusing John Slezer's *Theatrum Scotiae* (1693, reprinted 1979) and if possible an excursion to the Map Room in the National Library of Scotland in Edinburgh, where the visitor is rewarded with a marvellous array of maps and plans drawn by the draughtsmen in the office of the Board of Ordnance, who contributed so much to the construction of these forts against the Jacobites.

Index

(Numbers in **bold** indicate illustrations)